Praise for Coney Island Crackpots

"Zigun is a New York City culture hero, who single handedly brought Coney Island back from the dead, and tirelessly promotes American popular art. He founded the Mermaid Parade - homemade, artistic, glamorous, of the people. He is also an explosive and radical playwright. These Coney Island plays are raw, funny as hell, and have a backbone of the best kind of popular entertainment. They draw deeply on culture figures, the history of Coney Island, and are a slap in the face to more genteel theatrical fare, of whatever kind. They engage their audience directly, and take no prisoners. It's great news that this collection of Mr. Zigun's plays is now in print!"
-LEN JENKIN, Playwright

THE EDUCATION OF AL CAPONE AS IF TOLD BY JIMMY DURANTE

"...You can dodge the flying noodles or throw them back, but there's no escaping the action onstage... following 18-year-old hoodlum Al Capone as his nickname changes from "Babyface" to "Scarface." ... Jimmy Durante...plays enough piano to qualify the show as a mobster musical...It's all delivered with a wink and a laugh... but it's easy to get swept along and root for these charming characters.. but for all those moments of fun, there are just as many that might leave you squirming. Playwright Zigun does not let you forget that these mobsters were also monsters; innocent people get gunned down on and off stage..."
-BROOKLYN PAPER

"I would think these plays could be enjoyed by anyone without a stick up their ass and a healthy imagination. They're certainly not going to be for all markets. Plenty of theaters out there are addicted to middle-brow pablum. These plays definitely don't qualify on that count. But I think there are plenty of, particularly, smaller theaters out there for whom this type of material is exactly what they're looking for. It certainly gives actors, designers, directors the opportunity to genuinely stretch themselves, and to get as outrageous as they dare - something I don't think many get to do very often. I haven't been in an academic environment for a long time. But back when I was in college, this was precisely the kind of material that was red meat. College should be a place to stretch yourself, experiment, get as crazy and as out-there as you can. And these plays invite precisely that kind of limit-pushing. While I wouldn't describe these plays as "nostalgic" by any stretch of the imagination, Zigun's affection for an earlier time and place genuinely comes through. His cockeyed, slightly askew, funhouse mirror view of history ends up feeling more authentic than would be possible in a more straightforward approach. And, DAMN, doesn't Zigun nail Coney's spirit - these plays reek of sand in your shoes, sea air, hot dogs on the griddle, and sideshow attractions. He's a true chronicler of a unique time and place, and I can imagine artists seizing on his unique perspective and running with it!"

-STEVEN PATTERSON, Bridge Street Theatre

"Dick D. Zigun's plays provoke. They resonate. Zigun puts characters together in unique and unpredictable ways, and I'll bet you'll laugh as well as marvel."
-DAVID COPELIN, Playwright

"These six highly theatrical plays are perfect for young theater companies looking to investigate the wild events and colorful characters that make up our rich folklore."
-CASEY CHILDS, Primary Stages Company

"A wonderful souvenir of a self-created icon's theatrical adventures! Early obsessed by the spirit of P.T. Barnum, deeply influenced by Dada, the Surrealists, and such sui generis artists like him as Charles Ludlam and Richard Foreman, not to mention *Mad* magazine and other mind-rotting comics, and very early to the now-ubiquitous immersive theater scene, Dick D. Zigun channeled his profound love and deep historical knowledge of Coney Island and its denizens, plus a wicked sense of humor and trenchant sociopolitical insights, into his "Six Weird American Plays." How lucky we are to be invited to this funny but disturbingly disorienting party! Anyone with even a passing interest in Coney Island and its influence on entertainment in the United States and, indeed, around the world, will cherish this book, as will those interested in off-kilter theatrical experimentation. Students of the stage will find much to surprise and delight them, and professionals may well want to make hay with these scripts in their own off-the-beaten-path venues. "

-STEVEN SAMUEL, Manager/Actor, Ridiculous Theatrical Company; Producing Artistic Director/Publisher of The Sublime Theater & Press.

THE RIDE INSPECTOR'S NIGHTMARE

"...bloody interactive show about an 80-year-old man reliving his past through horrific drug-induced nightmares. Prepare for a Jackson Pollock–esque splattering of blood, guts and sickening sounds at this violently fun show..."
-TIME OUT

"In this kickass, carnival plays collection, Dick D. Zigun flips Coney Island into a perverse funhouse where spectacle, memory, and appetite crash. The keystone work, *Gorky Denouncing Dreamland*,adapts Maxim Gorky's 1905 prose into a stage-poem of lightbulbs and papier-mâché Hell, x-raying amusement as a two-sided cash register—pay to sin / pay to repent—and exposing spectatorship as ourown dark cruelty. It is the book's masterstroke: a lucid, unsentimental indictment of purchased pleasure quietly powering every moment of the American circus. What Divine did for John Waters' Baltimore; Everett Quinton for Charles Ludlam's Theatre of the Ridiculous; Carmen Maura for early Almodóvar's Madrid; Kate Manheim for Richard Foreman's Ontological-Hysteric Theater; and the Hilton sisters for Tod Browning's sideshow cinema—Zigun does for Coney Island: he baptizes a forgotten world, cultivates it, and makes its dreamscape contradictions sing well past midnight."
-ALLAN HAVIS, Playwright

"Dick Zigun is an iconoclastic playwright who pushes the form by exploring the intersections of entertainment, class, political corruption, and the glories of human frailty. He focuses his prescient perceptions through the lens of his beloved Coney Island, honing an image of a Brechtian Vaudeville. His plays are peopled by the denizens of sideshows and casinos, like a George Grosz painting Nazis and the "degenerates" they fear. H.L. Mencken was one of the greatest American journalists. Mencken was also a social critic. Dick Zigun is the H.L. Mencken of our time, reporting on the decline of the empire.

On the one hand, nothing is too weird for college drama students. On the other hand, Zigun's not for a general audience; he's a niche writer. I know that I'm not telling him anything he doesn't already know. Dick Zigun is the Félicien Rops of alternative theatre.

Zigun's writing is free associative, for example, in the Gorky script from a cage of bears to:
"In my circus dream I am a performing bear. I do impressions of Lenin and Mark Twain...the Czarina and Rasputin...of President Teddy Bear Roosevelt". Zigun always lifts his language into a poet's theatre. Zigun is creating an constellation of images in which the Russian orbits with the American. The Russian Bear greets Mark Twain, and sometimes they collide and merge, such as "President Teddy Bear Roosevelt." In the Al Capone script the play is a frame for the live performance of vintage music, such as: "Orchestra Pianist in the style of the 1921 recording of the Original Dixieland Jazz Band: Bow Wow Blues Everyone barks like a dog and makes animal sounds. "What a montage: Cruelty and Playfulness. Zigun is unearthing dark material; the urge to kill conflated with the urge to play. Durante and Clara Bow are not your usual comedians. Zigun has composed a cultural and political indictment disguised as the broad entertainment of a saloon."
-MATTHEW McGUIRE, Playwright

Coney Island Crackpots

Six Weird American Plays

Dick D. Zigun

Outside Talker Press (an imprint of Vaudevisuals Press)

Cover design by Jason Lonon

Layout by Nathan Wakefield

ISBN: 979-8-9989257-4-0

Library of Congress Control Number: 2026907106

Published by Outside Talker Press, an imprint of Vaudevisuals Press.

www.outsidetalkerpress.com

Contents

Acknowledgements

THANKS TO:

Darren, for suggesting this book;

Jim for publishing this book;

Norman for documenting so many plays;

Chicava for collaborating on the book;

And Jen for getting me thru every day and every page.

Foreword

A COUPLE OF DRAMATURGS SITTING AROUND TALKING ABOUT *CONEY ISLAND CRACKPOTS*

[Jack] We are jumping into a truly unique and genuinely bizarre stack of sources today. It's a collection of plays by Dick D. Zigun, and they're all centered around this historical, glittering, and well, often grotesque playground that is Coney Island, New York.

[Jill] That's right. And for those who don't know, Zigun is, I mean, he's often called the unofficial mayor of Coney Island. He's the founder of Coney Island USA, the organization behind the famous Mermaid Parade. He's a huge figure in the American sideshow revival. And these plays, yeah, they're not historical documentaries. They are high concept theatrical funhouse mirrors reflecting American culture.

[Jack] Absolutely. The sources really show how Zigun takes these icons. I mean, figures like the Russian revolutionary Maxim Gorky, the legendary gangster Al Capone.

[Jill] And Bettie Page.

[Jack] Bettie Page, yeah. He forces them to confront their destiny under the flashing cheap lights of the Brooklyn Beach. It's immersion spectacle.

[Jill] And a ton of historical distortion, all of it used to critique, you know, American morality.

[Jack] He's taking the famous and the infamous, mixing them up with a splatter of violence and a heavy dose of irony.

[Jill] Our mission here is to reveal what seems to be the central insight that Coney Island is the essential crucible where the American dream is manufactured and usually immediately corrupted.

[Jack] We're starting with a surprisingly literary source set in what, 1905. It's a play called Gorky Denouncing Dreamland, adapted from Maxim Gorky's essay Boredom.

[Jill] It's an incredibly powerful opening. So the play is set with Gorky and his partner Maria Andreyeva addressing the amusement park workers union in December 1905. And you have to remember, Gorky was this major socialist writer and revolutionary. He came to America expecting to find, you know, a kind of utopia.

[Jack] And Andreyeva, she beautifully sets up that expectation, right? She describes her first sight of Dreamland at night.

[Jill] Right.

[Jack] Yeah, it's this magnificent magical vision.

[Jill] She calls it a city of fire, a cobweb spun of gold. A fantastic cauldron of rich molten gold. It sounds like this overwhelming, perfect mechanical paradise.

[Jack] But Gorky, he just immediately tears that down. He shows that the beauty is completely manufactured and temporary.

[Jill] Right. He talks about how the vision just collapses in the harsh clarifying daylight. She says, "The sun slaps a man in the face with the true facts of life, and all you see are these flimsy white buildings covered in blue fog and gray smoke. It's just a stage set."

[Jack] And Gorky is furious about this, this deception. He finds the electric lights, even at night, they cast what he calls a dismal denuding light.

[Jill] That just illuminates stupid, dismal ugliness. The whole thing for him is not grand. It's an absurd jumble of straight lines and wood, a cheap, hastily constructed ghoul house.

[Jack] So his condemnation is, it's really a critique of American manufactured leisure. Yeah. Of, you know, exploitative capitalism.

[Jill] Exactly. It's not just a physical critique, it's a moral one. And that's where he gets to that famous line, "In America, the amusement parks are the opiate of the people."

[Jack] And he points out this cynical contradiction in the design of it all. It's designed, he argues, to extract money from the working man's paycheck. On one side of the boardwalk, you have an attraction of educational terror, warning people about hell.

[Jill] Right, painted dark red with paper fire. It's a literal sign, "Do not sin."

[Jack] But then right across the way, there's the dance hall, pushing the exact opposite.

[Jill] Sin, for sin is pleasant.

[Jack] The contradiction is the business model itself. Pay to sin, pay to be warned about sinning, pay for cheap entertainment and just forget the brutal monotony of your life.

[Jill] And here's where Gorky's critique gets really dark. This is the detail that, I mean, it really sticks with you. He describes the audience surrounding an organ grinder's monkey and child.

[Jack] Oh, this part is just brutal.

[Jill] It's the most visceral example of the moral ugliness he sees. The mother monkey is desperately shielding her infant, while the audience members, and he calls them white-skinned savages, they're poking sticks and umbrellas at the mother and child. They find it frightfully amusing. It's just cruel fun. And he makes the point of saying that not a single woman protests this, this petty spectacle. Yeah. It's the audience's own appetite for minor cruelty that reveals how hollow the whole thing is .

[Jack] Yeah. And it leads to his incredibly cynical, but also powerful conclusion. He says, "One thing there is good for a man like me in the city of fire. You can drink in hatred to your soul's content. Hatred of the power of stupidity." He basically leaves Coney Island fueled by contempt.

[Jill] That sets the stage perfectly. So if Gorky hated the American audience for their appetite for cruel fun, let's see how Zigun answers that challenge. He basically forces the audience into the cruel fun itself. Here's where it gets really interesting. We move from uh highbrow Russian critique to lowbrow American criminality. The education of Al Capone as if told by Jimmy Durante.

[Jack] This play is set in 1917 at the Harvard Inn, which was a real Coney Island saloon right behind Nathan's, and it immediately just ups the ante on audience interaction and, well, aggression.

[Jill] The atmosphere is crucial here. It's billed as a dirty dinner theater Brechtian cabaret.

[Jack] Uh-huh.

[Jill] And for anyone unfamiliar, Brechtian theater is um it's deliberately non-realistic. It breaks the fourth wall, constantly reminding you that you're watching a critique, not just entertainment.

[Jack] It's supposed to disrupt your comfort, force you to think about the, you know, the political or social context of what you're seeing.

[Jill] And Zigun does this literally with food and violence.

[Jack] Yep. The program warns patrons about profanity, anachronisms, ethnic stereotypes, and my favorite, ballistic pasta.

[Jill] Which is exactly what happens when an 18-year-old Al Capone shows up. He's wild, he's demanding, and he eats linguini like an animal, sharpening knives, using brass knuckles as utensils, and critically, spitting spaghetti onto the audience members.

[Jack] You're made physically part of the spectacle, part of the mess.

[Jill] You, the listener, you become complicit in the birth of this American monster.

[Jack] And he's there demanding to see the boss, Frankie Yale, who he compliments as a cold-hearted bloodthirsty killer.

[Jill] Yale runs the show. He operates a secret society called Skull and Bones, which is just the local name for the Italian Black Hand. The initiation ritual, of course, requires murder. And Yale starts teaching the young Capone his core rules for success in America.

[Jack] Like, the only good rat is a dead rat.

[Jill] And don't talk to the cops unless the cop's with me.

[Jack] The climax, of course, is the birth of Scarface. Capone gets into this violent knife fight with a guy named Frank Galluccio, and Galluccio slashes Capone's face three times with a pocket knife yelling, "I'm trying to slit your throat."

[Jill] And the sources are explicit about this. Blood squirts from Capone's cheek and lands on the audience. He ends up with 73 stitches and is officially renamed Scarface by Yale, who insists that scars and tattoos are necessary to earn respect in their world. This is his real Coney Island education.

[Jack] It perfectly fulfills Gorky's earlier observation, but with a, you know, an American twist. Gorky saw the audience craving cruel fun, poking a monkey. Zigun shows the American cultural machine serving up actual blood and violence for profit. It blurs the line between the spectacle and the consumer.

[Jill] And Capone leaves shortly after for Chicago, just declaring, "Fugget about Brooklyn, it's yours."

[Jack] So Coney Island is the site of American criminality being formalized and celebrated. Now let's turn to the making of an entirely different kind of icon, Bettie Page, in the 1950s play Becoming Bettie Page.

[Jill] Yeah.

[Jack] This is where celebrity is born from trauma.

[Jill] That's the core tension of this piece, absolutely. Bettie Page, before she was Bettie Page, was a Nashville girl, a former teacher, divorced. She was working as a secretary in Haiti before moving to New York City, and she gets discovered on the Coney Island beach by an NYPD sergeant who also happens to be a photographer, Jerry Tibbs.

[Jack] And her motivation for modeling isn't fame. It's it's safety, which is just heartbreaking.

[Jill] Mhm.

[Jack] She confesses to Tibbs that she needs protection. She tells him this horrifying story about being assaulted under the Delancey Street Bridge after trusting a stranger who asked her to dance.

[Jill] And it's that need for control over her image that drives the transformation. Tibbs immediately critiques her look. He says, "The camera doesn't like the glare on your big forehead," and he suggests cutting bangs.

[Jack] And she does it immediately, just right there. And this simple action creates her iconic, recognizable look that instantly transforms her into the confident, perfect pin-up model we all know. Coney Island gives her the disguise she needs.

[Jill] But the disguise, I mean, it immediately leads to further exploitation. Tibbs introduces her to Irving Klaw's world, the mail order cheesecake pin-ups, paying $100 an hour for specialized stockings, stilettos, and bondage scenes, which quickly escalates. She visits a raunchy live performance at a place called Tirza's Wine Bath. It was so notorious that a New York judge called it the most indecent skin show in New York.

[Jill] She becomes all the rage in the sweaty fetish mags, but the career built on controlling her own images, well, it's abruptly ended by the very moral panic Gorky warned about. She gets ripped down by the Kefauver Senate Committee investigation into pornography.

[Jack] Wait, let's pause on the Kefauver Committee for a second. This wasn't just some simple arrest. The Kefauver hearings in the 50s were these huge Senate investigations. They were supposed to be about organized crime and juvenile delinquency, but they quickly spiraled into this moral crusade against comic books, pin-ups, anything deemed obscene.

[Jill] Exactly. It wasn't really about law, it was about public image and morality policing, often driven by political motivations. So the moment Bettie achieves this total fame and notoriety, the manufactured leisure industry just turns on her. The authorities dismantle the very persona she created for protection. Coney Island provided the stage for her spectacular rise and her spectacular fall.

[Jack] So what does this all mean when you mix a Russian revolutionary's hatred, a gangster's initiation, and a pin-up's transformation? We finish by exploring the central archive of this strange American culture, the Coney Island Wax Museum.

[Jill] We're talking about Lillie's World in Wax. It opened in 1927, run by Lillie Beatrice Santangelo, who was sometimes called New York's Madame Tussaud. Lillie insisted her museum was art and that it teaches you the good things in life and that crime doesn't pay.

[Jack] But the inventory, it's a catalog of moral chaos. The juxtaposition is the entire point. You walk in and you see John Lennon in a post-assassination tribute in his white suit and sneakers, and you see Muhammad Ali, revered cultural icons.

[Jill] And right next to them are the American martyrs, JFK, MLK, RFK, who Lillie portrays as alive in the White House together making plans in the civil rights days. It's a wax vision of this idealized lost American hope.

[Jack] But that dreamscape is immediately contaminated by pure graphic horror. Standing near these peaceful heroes are the era's most notorious killers. Richars Speck, who murdered eight student nurses.

[Jill] And John Christie, the full moon strangler, displayed in the act of choking a blonde victim.

[Jack] And then there's the just medically bizarre. Like Lina Medina, the world's youngest mother, who gave birth at five years old, displayed next to the Duke of Windsor, who gave up his throne for love. What is the common thread here?

[Jill] Sensationalism. The sensationalism of transgression. It doesn't matter if you are a victim, a hero, or a mass murderer. If your story sells tickets, you belong in Lillie's world.

[Jack] So Lillie's stated mission, crime does not pay, it just completely dissolves when the most popular exhibits are the biggest criminals and the most tragic victims. It's an American contradiction. We say we value peace and genius, but we pay to stare at murder and medical oddities.

[Jill] And get this, here's where the surreal Coney Island just permeates American culture in the most literal way possible. Lillie's voice was accidentally secretly dubbed onto the full album version of John Lennon's final song, Watching the Wheels.

[Jack] No way. That garbled cryptic part at the end of the track, released on the Double Fantasy album after he died, that's the real life carnival spiel of a wax museum owner.

[Jill] That's it. It's the sound of the grotesque American carnival bleeding directly into the final work of a global peace icon. It's proof that the chaos of the boardwalk is inextricable from the machinery of celebrity.

[Jack] Wow. Okay, so to bring us full circle on the price of manufactured fun, we have to look at the Ride Inspector's Nightmare. This one explicitly ties the failure of the infrastructure to the trauma of the employees.

[Jill] Yeah, this is a bloody interactive horror play. It's set in the NYC Department of Buildings locker room, where an inspector, Patty McKay, relives these drug-induced nightmares. It's a direct critique of the shoddy construction Gorky noticed all the way back in 1905.

[Jack] Patty and the Deputy Chief Inspector Manny Mandelbaum, they swap stories that aren't dry reports. They're gruesome anecdotes of catastrophic failures, like a customer losing his head on the Jumbo Jet ride.

[Jill] Or an arm being severed while grasping a hot dog at Nathan's, and the arm lands right on the grill.

[Jack] The absurdity and the horror are completely inseparable.

[Jill] Another detail is a customer's hair being completely ripped out on the go-kart track. These are the human and mechanical failures hidden behind the cheap thrill ticket.

[Jack] And the horror becomes deeply personal when Patty's wife, Mary McKay, appears in his nightmare holding their dead baby. She confronts him, revealing their son died on a ride Patty himself signed off on. She calls him a murderer. This is the price of signing off on that cheap construction.

[Jill] He's ultimately sentenced by the judge, who condemns the ride inspector to death by the guillotine for DWI, dreaming while intoxicated. But the irony is the nightmare ends with him waking up, realizing you can't die in your own dream. He assures the audience the rides in Coney Island are safe. Nobody dies in the end, except for an occasional audience member at his creep show.

[Jack] The joke being the danger is real, but the theatrical experience is the only thing guaranteed to be safe. So what these deep dives show is that Coney Island is the essential American crucible. It's a place where dreams of celebrity, wealth, and spiritual escape are constantly being fractured by grotesque realities and the ruthless nature of show business.

[Jill] Exactly. Zigun's whole approach is to cut history and culture up and serve it back to us, sometimes literally, with the ballistic pasta and squirted stage blood. He shows us that the search for sensation, whether it's through pin-ups, violence, or freak show displays, is what fuels the entire American entertainment mechanism.

[Jack] We've seen Capone get Scarface, Bettie Page get her bangs and immediate exploitation, and Gorky get his lifetime of hatred all under those cheap dazzling lights. The wax museum offered education alongside horror, teaching that crime does not pay, yet the biggest stars are the ones who committed the crimes or died tragically sensational deaths.

[Jill] These plays suggest that the American audience, those white-skinned savages Gorky hated, are perpetually drawn to the spectacular and the grotesque. We crave the chaos. We want to see the famous displayed next to the infamous because it makes us feel like we understand the rules of this unpredictable, bizarre cultural melting pot.

[Jack] So if our greatest cultural icons and our worst criminals are displayed side by side in the same hall of fame, in Lillie's World in Wax, what does that say about what America truly values and what kind of entertainment we crave? Think about that the next time you hear a tragic or sensational story in the news and just how quickly it becomes a piece of profitable entertainment.

(Jack and Jill, the real dramaturgs who held this conversation, wish to remain anonymous.)

GORKY DENOUNCING DREAMLAND

Adapted by DICK D. ZIGUN

From MAXIM GORKY'S Essay: BOREDOM (1907)

PRODUCTION HISTORY

GORKY DENOUNCING DREAMLAND was originally workshopped under the title BORE-DOM; by Coney Island USA at Sideshows by the Seashore, Brooklyn, NY opening December 19, 1992, and closed January 17, 1993 after 20 performances. The workshop was funded in part by The National Endowment for The Arts, NYS Council On The Arts and NYC Department of Cultural Affairs.

Directed by Dick Zigun; Sets by Paolo Spina; Costumes by Kate Morrison; Lights by Joseph Errante.

CAST

Yevgeny Gluschevsky (Maxim Gorky); Oksana Volgina (Andreyeva); Tony Ferero (Tony The Carpenter)
Now retitled, the play received a Brooklyn Showcase Premiere at The Coney Island Museum Brooklyn, NY in 2015 produced by Coney Island USA partially funded by NYC Cultural Affairs and performed by the Funhouse Philosophers Theater Company.
Directed by James Rana. Production Design: Kate Dale.

CAST

Chris DePierro (Gorky); Atalanta Siegelas (Andreyeva); Luis Michaels (Tony The Carpenter)

CAST OF HISTORICAL CHARACTERS

TONY THE CARPENTER
GORKY
ANDREYEVA

TIME

1905

PLACE

Meeting Hall in Coney Island

SET DESIGN

Podium with Seal of Amusement Park Workers Union, Local 105

PAPER MACHE PROPS

Model of Columbus's boat

Spyglass telescope

Magnifying glass

Devil mask and pitchfork

Angel strung up by wire with wooden trumpet covered with gilt paper

Darwinian chart showing Man and Monkey and Theory of Evolution

OTHER PROPS

World map, retro American and Communist flags, miscellaneous storage of amusement park objects, dress table with tablecloth from the meeting hall.

Miniature skyline of Coney Island for upper balcony platform. Skyline with white Christmas lights. Lots and lots of little lights.

(Lights up on stage and podium TONY THE CARPENTER enters.)

TONY THE CARPENTER

Hey there, folks. Nice turnout. Sit down. Sit down. A lot of you people already know me...for those of you who don't... I'm Tony. I was the head carpenter when we built Dreamland Amusement Park two years ago... and this year I'm out of a job! And I bet a few of you are out of a job! My dear, dear working-class brothers and sisters... cashiers and carpenters of Coney Island... welcome to the December meeting of Amusement Park Workers Union Local 15. It warms my heart to see such a strong turnout in frigid December. Our rich bosses: Tilyou—Thompson—Dundy—and Reynolds are all out of town; off on vacation. What mischief we might make if we were better organized in Coney Island, yes? I call this meeting to order! I make a motion to dispense with the minutes! Etc., etc., pay you union due, etc. Thank you very much. This month we were going to plan the organization of the 300 midgets living in the Lilliputian Village but we'll do that next month...because tonight we have special guests! Maxim Gorky, the famous Russian writer, the heroic revolutionary poet of the peasants and workers , as you know he is visiting New York this year with Maria Andreyeva—

OFFSTAGE HECKLER

WHORE!

TONY THE CARPENTER

Our GUESTS: Gorky and Maria Andreyeva, a good woman revolutionary and an actress with the Moscow Art Theatre. As you know, they were recently kicked out of their hotel room...the front page newspaper scandals...they've been staying at a good comrade's house out on Staten Island.....they've been bored out of their minds...I invited them out to Coney Island...I asked him to speak...we've been goofing around with papier mache for some props...etc., etc. without further introduction I am honored to welcome Maxim Gorky and Maria Andreyeva!

(GORKY and ANDREYEVA enter. He mingles with the audience. She stands at the podium. She taps a baton.)

GORKY

We must begin now. I will sign more autographs later.

ANDREYEVA

All of a sudden: Abracadabra!

(GORKY wanders the audience with a papier mache ship.)

GORKY

If there were a God, God would whisper to his prophet, little Gorky, "You think you are Columbus discovering America."

CHRIS DePIERRO as Maxim Gorky with a papier-mâché model of Columbus's boat. Photo by Norman Blake.

ATALANTA SIEGELAS as Maria Andreyeva watching CHRIS DePIERRO as Maxim Gorky discover America. Photo by Norman Blake.

ANDREYEVA

When night falls a fantastic city of fire rises from the ocean and reaches for the sky. Thousands of glowing sparks glimmer in the darkness

(LIGHT CUE: Christmas lights.)

tracing the outlines of fairytale castles, palaces and temples against the black sky. It is like a cobweb spun of gold, quivering in the air — a translucent pattern of flames, hanging motionless, admiring its own beauty in the sea. This city of fire is enchanting, it is magic, it is incomprehensible; it burns but it is never consumed. If you could only imagine the heavens, the ocean, the city of fire! The sky above glowing in red, the waters below reflecting its brilliance...it all merges, it blends, it all melts into a fantastic caldron of rich molten gold. Strange thoughts fill the mind at the sight of these lights. In the halls of these magic castles there must be weird music.

(SOUND CUE: Weird heavenly music.)

Soft music. Proud music. Floating music the likes of which no man ever heard. I imagine waves of melodies collecting the best thoughts on earth and then throwing out shooting stars—

(LIGHT CUE: Mirror Ball.)

dazzling sparks, dancing with one another, giving birth to new flames and new thoughts. It must be here, near this velvety darkness, that I imagine a huge cradle woven of gold thread and flowers and stars. The giant cradle rocks gently on the breast of the ocean. Here, in the city of fire, the sun itself sleeps until dawn.

(GORKY ditches boat.)

(LIGHT CUE: Blackout.)

(SOUND CUE: Sound out.)

All of a sudden: Abracadabra!

(GORKY reveals a spyglass and GORKY and ANDREYEVA are now passengers on the boat.)

This is real Gorky! The sun slaps a man in the face with the true facts of life! Daylight turns the city of fire and the magic castles into a handful of flimsy white buildings. The blue fog of the ocean mixes with grey smoke from New York City...the white buildings are enveloped in a transparent veil... it all becomes a mirage. It beckons alluringly, the mirage quivers —— and promises something splendid and smooth.

All of a sudden: Abracadabra!

(SOUND CUE: Industrial city.)

I hear a hum in the background. The city sounds fill the air with a loud, hungry roar. This is a raucous noise, it agitates both the air and the soul. An endless bellow of industrial iron. The ugly sound of New York. The constant crushing sound of life after life being ground down by the power of gold — the cold, cynical whistle of the Yellow Devil — this is the sound that chases people away from an earth befouled by the stinking body of the city. And so the American people run and they flee to the beach by the sea where they have built beautiful white buildings that promise them rest, that promise them peace.

(ANDREYEVA turns her back. GORKY continues in Russian.)

It cannot be translated!

(GORKY goes to her and proposes marriage in Russian.)

...I am seized with a desire...he is seized with a desire...we are seized with a desire...I am seized with the desire to live on this island. I long to go and touch the fabric and textures, to stretch out in the luxurious folds and feast my eyes on the wide horizon where the white birds dart about swiftly and noiselessly, where the ocean and the sky take a nap in the tanning rays of the sun...it sounds like a honeymoon...This is Coney Island...

GORKY

This is Coney IS—Land!

(They cross to the desk. She hands him a newspaper and a magnifying glass.)

ANDREYEVA

Every Monday the New York newspapers run headlines that proudly announce something like:

GORKY

"Three Hundred Thousand People Visited Coney Island Yesterday. Twenty Three Children Were Lost"...there must be something doing there...

(He lights a cigarette. She steals it, she puffs it, she puts it out and tosses the cig into the spittoon. He retrieves it.)

It's very expensive!

ANDREYEVA

He's a savage!... he's my savage... It's a long journey... it is a very, very long ride by trolley car through the dusty and noisy streets of Brooklyn before one sets eyes on the dazzling splendour of Coney Island. And, indeed, from the very first moment a man stands before the entrance to this city of fire, he is blinded.

(LIGHT CUE: Spinners.)

The eye is assaulted by hundreds of thousands of cold white lights and for a long time you cannot make out a thing for all this sparkling dust round about. Everything whirls and dazzles, everything blends into a whirlwind of fiery foam.

(LIGHT CUE: Pulsing Lights.)

The tourist is stunned, his mind is erased by all this brilliance, all thought is driven out of his head and he becomes a little speck in the crowd. People wander aimlessly, devoid of will, intoxicated by light. A dull white fog penetrates their brain, a feeling of greedy anticipation envelopes their souls. Hypnotized by the glitter, the crowd of people pours, like a dark stream, into the dark frontiers of the night.

(GORKY stands on a chair and plays with the hanging light.)

(LIGHT CUE: Lights stop pulsing.)

Everywhere you go, electric light bulbs shed a cold, garish gleam. Light bulbs are attached to the poles and the walls, to the window frames and roofs of the buildings, they outline the tall chimney of the power station, they burn every cornice, they poke the eye with a sharp needle of indifferent sparkle. The people blink and, smiling stupidly, drag themselves along the ground like the heavy links in some tangled chain...

(LIGHT CUE: Christmas Lights.)

A man must make a great effort not to get lost in this crowd, not to be overwhelmed by his amazement — an amazement in which there is neither joy nor delight. But if a man has the will to individualize himself, he discovers that these millions of bulbs cast a dismal, denuding light that, while hinting at the possibility of beauty, only illuminate the stupid, dismal ugliness all around. This magic city, a dreamland from afar, is revealed to be an absurd jumble of straight

lines in wood, a cheap, hastily constructed dollhouse for the amusement of children. There is only an ugly variety to these many white buildings, and not one of them with even a suggestion of beauty. They are all built of wood, and all smeared over with peeling white paint, which gives them all the appearance of suffering from the same skin disease. The tallest towers and the low colonnades stretch in two deadly even lines insipidly pressing upon each other. Everything is stripped naked and robbed by the impartial glare of the lights; the glare is everywhere and there are no shadows. Every single building stands like some gaping fool with his mouth hanging open. People eat, drink and smoke but the human voice is not heard. The air is filled with the hissing of the arc lamps, ragged fragments of music, the whistle of the peanut stands and the constant sputtering of sausage counters. All these sounds mingle into an irritating hum; as of some invisible chord. And when a human voice invades this endless chord, it sounds like a frightened whisper. Everything glitters, everything is insulting, everything dismal ugliness...

(GORKY lights a match.)

(LIGHT CUE: Blackout except podium and balcony.)

The soul is seized with a desire for a living, beautiful fire, a sublime flame, that would deliver the crowd from their slavery to glittering boredom that deafens their ears and dazzles their eyes. One would wish to set fire to all this prettiness, one wishes to burn and to dance and shout and sing and revel in a voluptuous feast of destruction of this deadly city of spiritual poverty...

(LIGHT CUE: Blackout.)

(SOUND CUE: Riot.)

(LIGHT CUE: Lights up.)

(TONY THE CARPENTER jumps up on stage and waves a red flag.)

TONY THE CARPENTER

Are you getting ready for our May Day Strike, Boys? A May Day Worker's Strike, Brothers and Sisters! We'll Strike! We'll march! We'll start a Revolution!

GORKY

Three hundred thousand people...three hundred thousand people...three hundred thousand people...

ANDREYEVA

Hundreds of thousands of people cram into this city. They swarm into the cages of the rides like black flies.

(GORKY begins to pantomime. ANDREYEVA plays with dolls.)

Pregnant women push on despite the weight of their bellies. Children walk about silent with their mouths hanging wide open, so wide—eyed, so dazzled. They look around them so intensely, so seriously upon this ugliness that they mistake for beauty that my soul aches with pity.

The men are all clean shaven, not a mustache, they look strangely alike and are all serious and fat. Most of the men bring their wives and their children along. They regard themselves as the benefactors of their families for they provide the family not only with bread but also take them out to the magnificent shows. The men themselves enjoy all the glitter but they are too serious to crack a smile, they keep their thin lips pressed together. They squint and they frown with the air of persons who cannot be impressed. Yet behind this mask of the man who has seen it all, one feels a burning desire to taste all the pleasures the town has to offer. And so these serious men, the benefactors of their families, trying very hard to mask the gleam in their eyes, clip up onto the backs of the merry-go-round horses

(SOUND CUE: Carnival rides.)

and carved elephants and dangle their feet, swing their legs, in excited anticipation of the wild pleasure found in flying over the rails. With a loud whoop a ride will toss them up to the top and with a whistle they drop down again and whirl through the air. This particular bumpy journey completed, the men stretch the skin tight on their faces again and move the family on to sample new pleasures…

(LIGHT CUE: Weird light.)

The rides are without end. There on the top of an iron tower two long white wings slowly flap up and then down. At the very end of each wing hangs a cage, and in these cages are people. When the wings soar heavenly skyward, the faces of the people in the cage grow painfully serious. With identical frightened expressions, they stare in round eyed silence as the earth shrinks beneath them. When the wing flaps down to the ground, all the faces blossom in smiles. There are always squeals of joyful delight. The sound reminds me of the merry yelp of a puppy dog when he is dropped onto the floor after having been held up in the air by the scruff of the neck. Boats fly though the air around the top of another tower; a third revolves and sets in motion some sort of iron balloon; a fourth and a fifth they all move, they all glitter, they all beckon the people with the silent shout of their lights. Everything swings, squeals, booms and bellows turning the heads of the people this way then that. They grow dizzy, they grow dull, their nerves are exhausted and tortured by the maze and the motion of lights.

(LIGHT CUE: Illuminate the lip of the steps.)

Wide eyes grow wider as if the brain were turning pale, drained of blood by the weird turmoil of all this white, glittering wood. The end result is a boredom, the boredom that crawls out from under the rock of self—disgust, whirling round and around in a slow circle of agony. It drags into its melancholy dance tens of thousands of faceless lost people and sweeps them up as the wind sweeps the rubbish on the streets…a random will—less heap over here…and then scatters them apart…only to sweep them together once more together again…

(LIGHT CUE: Blackout.)

(LIGHT CUE: Lights up.)

ANDREYEVA

On the inside of the buildings the people seek even more pleasures; but these are serious pleasures; inside, everything is supposed to be educational. And what is the people's favorite attraction?

GORKY

Let's go to HELL!

(He opens a trap door in the stage. Red ribbons of fire blow up from beneath the floor.)

...educational terror...educational punishment...do not break the Ten Commandments!

(He puts on a Devil's mask.)

ANDREYEVA

Hell is made out of papier-mâché and painted dark red. Everything in Hell is on fire

GORKY

Paper Fire!

CHRIS DePIERRO as Maxim Gorky as The Devil. Photo by Norman Blake

ANDREYEVA

And the whole place stinks with the dirty odor of grease.

GORKY

Hell is very badly done! The village idiot should demand his money back!

ANDREYEVA

Hell is found in a cave...a cave scattered with rocks...the room is quite dark with a red light here and there.

GORKY

On top of the biggest rock sits SATAN who is wearing scarlet tights. He is contorting his red face into grimaces. He is rubbing his hands together like a man who has just brought off a good business deal. I am thinking: he must be very uncomfortable sitting on top of a paper rock that is cracking and bending underneath him...but SATAN is a good actor and pretends not to notice. He concentrates on his band of devils below who are getting ready to torture the sinners.

(ANDREYEVA puts on her hat and looks at herself in a hand mirror.)

ANDREYEVA

Over here is a young girl who has just bought herself a new hat and admires herself in the mirror. A couple of small and apparently very horny devils sneak up on her from behind and seize her by the arms! She cries out! "Help me! Help me!"

(ANDREYEVA steps into a second trap door and is also in a pit of Hell with red ribbons of fire.)

GORKY

But too late!

ANDREYEVA

The horny little devils throw her into a trap door, and she slides down a chute into a pit in the middle of the cave. The young girl, along with the mirror and the new hat, all burn in Hell!

GORKY

A young man drinks a glass of whiskey—

(TONY stumbles around drinking. GORKY grabs him and they both go off stage and grab drinks of Vodka.)

ANDREYEVA

And those little devils grab the drinking man and down he goes through another trap door in the floor of the stage.

(Both GORKY and ANDREYEVA stand in trap doors.)

It is stuffy in Hell. The actors who play the devils are skinny and stupid. They are worn out and exhausted. The hours are long. The script is obvious. They waste no time playing any scene with the sinners. Sinner after sinner just tossed through a trap door like so many logs of wood onto the fire. A few minutes of watching this educational show and an intelligent man want to shout:

GORKY

Enough of this bullshit! Why don't you go out on a strike, boys!

(LIGHT CUE: Out on trap doors and Hell.)

(They climb out of the trap doors.)

ANDREYEVA

But the Coney Island public watches this horror in silence with serious faces. A hefty young fellow with curly hair and wearing a priest's collar delivers a harangue in a deep voice of doom.

TONY THE CARPENTER

(Puts on a mask and stands on top of desk.)

THOU SHALL NOT KILL!

THOU SHALL NOT COMMIT ADULTERY!

ANDREYEVA

Pointing to Hell on the stage he declares that if boys do not want to fall victim to the bowlegged Satan in the red tights, they should not kiss girls to whom they are not married, because then the girls might become...bad women.

GORKY

Prostitutes!

ANDREYEVA

You cannot say "prostitutes". You cannot shout "bullshit".

GORKY

Prostitutes! Hypocrites! America! Ten commandments! Yellow devil! It is a sin to kiss young men without the blessing of the church because little boys and girls may be born as a result! It is a sin for prostitutes to steal money from the customer's pocket! Why? Why not? It is a sin to drink whiskey or vodka or liquids in general that get juices flowing! Thou shalt not visit saloons! Go to church! Church is better for the soul...and church is cheaper...hypocrites!

(He takes another drink of vodka.)

(Improvisation about the American newspaper called THE WORLD which denounced GORKY and ANDREYEVA living together without being married.)

ANDREYEVA

The actor who plays the preacher talks in a weary monotone. He himself does not seem to believe in the kind of life he has been instructed to preach. An intelligent man is tempted to find the owners of this educational amusement called Hell and tell them:

GORKY

Gentlemen! If you wish your morality play to have an effect of men's souls, at least equal to the effect of castor oil, you must pay your preachers and actors more money!

ANDREYEVA

All of a sudden:

(LIGHT CUE: On ANGEL's entrance.)

(She claps twice. TONY manipulates an angel crossing the stage on a pole.)

At the conclusion of this terrible performance, a disgustingly handsome angel appears from a corner of the cave. Strung up by a wire, it moves through the air across the entire cave holding a wooden trumpet between his teeth that has been pasted over with gilt paper.

GORKY

Catching sight of the angel, SATAN dives like a fish into the pit with the sinners. A crash is heard, the papier mache boulders roll down one against the other, and the actors playing the devils run off as fast as they can to take a coffee break. The curtain falls. The audience stands and they leave. A few, the brave ones, they can laugh. The majority are very serious. Perhaps they are thinking: "If Hell is so horrible...maybe it isn't worth sinning.

(LIGHT CUE: Hell out.)

ANDREYEVA

(Strolling.)

We move on. In the next building we are shown THE WORLD BEYOND THE GRAVE.

(TONY covers himself in a sheet and becomes a Ghost.)

GORKY

Badly dressed ghosts of the dead roam about aimlessly. You may wink at them but you must not pinch them...some of the ghosts have bad coughs, some ghosts chew tobacco and spit yellow saliva on the ground...many of these ghosts are clearly suffering from rheumatism.

ANDREYEVA

We move on. In another building we see THE FLOOD.

GORKY

Did you know that THE FLOOD was sent to punish the people on Earth for their sins...this building, that building, all the shows in this city have one purpose: to instruct the people how they will be punished after death for their sins...to teach them to live on this Earth and be humble and meek...obey the laws...obey the church...obey the Czar...

(TONY becomes a Preacher.)

TONY THE CARPENTER

Thou Shall Not...Thou Shall Not...

GORKY

thou shall not! THREE HUNDRED THOUSAND PEOPLE...Thou shall not! Three hundred thousand people in Coney Island...thou shall not realize that the overwhelming majority of the public are the working people!

(LIGHT CUE: Desk only.)

(ANDREYEVA goes to desk and removes hat.)

ANDREYEVA

But it is necessary to make money, Maxim...in every corner of this city of fire, in every corner on Earth...the greed laughs at hypocrisy and lies. Of course, the greed is hidden and, of course, it is dull but the greed, it is also for the people.

GORKY

For the people?

ANDREYEVA

The amusement park is organized as a profitable business, as a means to extract a working man's pay from his pocket. The business has a passion for gold.

GORKY

It is repulsive...it is despicable...it is a slimy marsh of glittering boredom.

ANDREYEVA

The people feed on it.

GORKY

In America, the amusement parks are the opiate of the people. The buildings on the right terrorize them with the horrors of eternal damnation: Do not sin! It is dangerous! The spacious dance hall on the left features young single women waltzing in slow circles and here, everything about this establishment urges:

ANDREYEVA & GORKY

Sin! For sin is pleasant!

(GORKY kisses ANDREYEVA passionately. They dance. TONY hoists a mirror ball attached to a long pole. It reflects the spotlight.)

ANDREYEVA

Blinded by the lights...tempted by the cheap but dazzling luxury...intoxicated by the noise...the people swing in a slow dance of weary boredom...swing to the left and we sin with the merchants of vice...swing to the right and we repent with the preachers of virtue...

(LIGHT CUE: Podium only.)

(GORKY sings a song as they dance.)

GORKY

Life is organized so that people shall work six days in the week and on the seventh day, sin...and pay for their sins...and then confess...and then pay for the confession...and that's all...

(LIGHT CUE: Blackout.)

(LIGHT CUE: Lights up on GORKY at the podium. The rest of the stage is in darkness.)

GORKY

I have amusing Coney Island Dream. I have dream this same night about a circus in Coney Island. Thousands of snakes in the grass...the sky swarming with flies...insects and serpents come through every door of the circus...and turn into audience...is dream, please excuse. Before show, audience loiters in front of the animal cages...chews tobacco...and spits!

(He spits into the brass spittoon.)

(SOUND CUE: Surreal circus music.)

Music...ringmaster...spotlight. In circus dream, the Russian actress Maria Andreyeva is strong lion tamer...with chair...whip...with gun!

(SOUND CUE: A loud gunshot.)

(LIGHT CUE: Lights come up on ANDREYEVA with smoking gun and with a whip and chair in her hands.)

ANDREYEVA

In Gorky's dream, Gorky is a big Indian tiger...roaring and snorting...teeth gnashing...paws slashi ng...ready to leap into the air and sink his claws into the flesh of Andreyeva with her whip...to tear her to pieces...to destroy her...

(LIGHT CUE: Lights out on ANDREYEVA.)

(GORKY leaves the stage runs into the audience and sits with audience.)

(LIGHT CUE: Lights out on stage and lights up on GORKY sitting in audience.)

GORKY

The audience waits...the audience wants to see blood and is waiting for blood...not out of a desire for vengeance...but out of curiosity...the audience desires blood...but the audience is

afraid...it both wants it and does not want it and in this dark struggle with itself...it experiences a pretty good time...the audience lives...

(LIGHT CUE: Lights down on the audience.)

(LIGHT CUE: Lights up on ANDREYEVA on stage with the whip.)

ANDREYEVA

Andreyeva cracks her whip and shouts like a madwoman! Gorky retreats to the back of the cage. He is sweating and relieved that in his dream he has survived...he smiles...he bows as to an idol.

(LIGHT CUE: Lights up on the podium.)

(GORKY back on stage at the podium.)

GORKY

The audience shouts and claps its hands and sighs — is it relief or is it regret? The audience melts into a slimy marsh or boredom. In Gorky's dream...Gorky has had too much to drink, and Gorky goes to the bathroom.

[He exits the stage and goes to a corner of the theater and pisses in a bucket. He yells out his lines, in Russian, from the toilet.

(ANDREYEVA translates.)

ANDREYEVA

Wouldn't it be a comic relief to see a drunk with a funny face come rolling along, singing, shouting. happy because he is drunk and sincerely wishing all good people the same from the bottom of his heart?

(Gorky flushes the toilet and returns, drunk, wishing everyone Merry Christmas, Happy Chanukah, Happy New Year! Happy May Day!)

(LIGHT CUE: Lights up on desk.)

GORKY

In my inebriated dream it is snowing...it is both summertime and Christmas time at the very same time. I am Santa Claus, ho, ho, ho, conducting the band at the circus. The music is bad...the band is tired and worn out...I am swinging a baton over the heads of the musicians who do not pay any attention to me...we are making music by beggars for the amusement of slaves...I rip the big tuba from the hands of its player and blow a blast long and loud and so terrible that all the snakes, all the insects run out of the prison driven by the horror of my wild sound...

(ANDREYEVA leads GORKY to the desk. GORKY puts on a Bear Mask. He sits underneath the desk.)

CHRIS DePIERRO as Maxim Gorky as The Bear. Photo by Norman Blake.

ANDREYEVA

Not far from the orchestra is a cage with the bears. One of the bears, a fat, brown bear with little crafty eyes, sits in the middle of the cage and shakes his head as if he were thinking: "I can accept this as rational only if I am shown that it has all been arranged deliberately in order to blind, deafen and deform the people. In that case, of course, the end justifies the means. But if the people sincerely come here to be amused...I have lost all faith in the mental sanity of three hundred thousand people!"

(LIGHT CUE: Lights on his "cage" under the desk only.)

GORKY

In my dream there are other bears in my cage. A momma bear and a poppa bear sit opposite each other and play chess. The baby bear expects nothing of this life and he has decided to go to bed. We are performing bears. The eyes of the audience loiter in front of my cage. I chew tobacco and spit. People silently poke sticks through the bars and jab me in the stomach and side, curious to see what will happen.

In my circus dream I am a performing bear. I do impressions of Lenin and Mark Twain...the Czarina and Rasputin...of President Teddy Bear Roosevelt.

(LIGHT CUE: Podium only.)

ANDREYEVA

And the people, in Gorky's dream, perhaps do a double take and then walk away to another attraction in Coney Island saying: "That's a dull animal..."

(LIGHT CUE: Blackout.)

(In the blackout the podium has been moved from the center of the stage.)

(LIGHT CUE: Lights up on GORKY and ANDREYEVA clutching each other center stage.)

(SOUND CUE: Organ grinder monkey music.)

GORKY

In front of the musicians is a post to which a pair of organ grinder's monkeys are tied by a thin chain.

ANDREYEVA

It is a mother

GORKY

—and her child. The infant clings to his mother's breast

ANDREYEVA

—the mother holds the baby in a tight embrace with one arm while the other is stretched out warily with the fingers crooked, ready to seize, to scratch, to strike. The mother's eyes express a despair, an anguished expectation of unavoidable insult and injury...a weary anger and resentment.

GORKY

The infant, cheeks pressed against the mother's breast, looks out of the corner of its eyes at the people. Apparently, the infant has been filled with dread from the very first day of its life and fear has petrified within it for the rest of its days.

ANDREYEVA

The mother bares her white teeth. Not even for a second does she remove the arm that holds his small body next to hers, yet with the other arm, she wards off continual sticks and umbrellas poked at her by the witnesses of her suffering.

GORKY

There are so many of them, these white—skinned savages, men and women, in straw hats and hats with feathers, and they all find it so frightfully amusing to see how skillfully mommy defends her child from the blows.

ANDREYEVA

There are so many of them, and each one of them is so anxious to strike, to pinch, to pull the monkey's tails, to jerk the chain around the neck, that we cannot manage them all.

GORKY

Now and again one of the musicians turns the stupid, brass bellow of his trumpet at the monkeys and overwhelms us with a deafening noise. The people laugh and nod to the musician in approval. A minute later he repeats his performance.

ANDREYEVA

There are women among the spectators. Some of them mothers, no doubt. But not one of the women utters a word of protest against this cruel fun. They enjoy it.

ANDREYEVA & GORKY

The torments of the mother monkey and the wild horror of the child.

(LIGHT CUE: Light change. They reveal a mock Darwinian evolution chart with drawings of monkeys and men.)

ANDREYEVA

Next to the monkeys and the bears and the lions is the cage of the elephant, an elderly gentleman. He watches the public and being a wise and sensible animal. He is thinking:

(SOUND CUE: Animal sounds.)

GORKY

Of course, of course, this is scum that has been swept together by the filthy broom of boredom. This species will mock their own prophets, so I have heard the old elephants say. But I am sorry for the monkey, anyway. I have also heard that these human beings, like the jackals and hyenas, sometimes tear each other to pieces...but that's no solace for the monkey...for the lowly human...for the pig...animals...forgive them...they know not what they do...

(LIGHT CUE: Blackout.)

(SOUND CUE: Boat and water sounds.)

(LIGHT CUE: Lights up on boat railing.)

(GORKY and ANDREYEVA both appear near the railing at the back of the theatre with the toy boat.)

GORKY

Well, well...bon voyage...dos vedonya...the boat is leaving...

ANDREYEVA

And so not so suddenly...abracadabra...when night falls – the fantastic city of fire blazes up from the ocean. It glows for a long time...its beauty...its brilliance...

GORKY

Its tens of thousands of grey people with colorless eyes creeping along like on the ragged clothes of a beggar!

(They continue to sail the boat, slowly, back to Europe. They speak in Russian only. Her words are soft. His are harsh. As the lights begin to fade on the actors, the lights outlining the miniature city come up one more time. One last comment for GORKY:)

One thing there is good for a man like me in this city of fire...you can drink in hatred to your soul's content...hatred sufficient to last a lifetime...hatred, my dear people, hatred of the power of stupidity!

(TONY THE CARPENTER waves goodbye. He sweeps the stage and turns off the lights.)

(LIGHT CUE: Blackout.)

(SOUND CUE: Exit music.)

THE END

THE EDUCATION OF AL CAPONE AS IF TOLD BY JIMMY DURANTE

By Dick D. Zigun

PRODUCTION HISTORY

Originally developed by CONEY ISLAND USA in Brooklyn, NY with funding from NYC Department of Cultural Affairs. Performed by the Funhouse Philosophers Theater Company.

First draft workshop under the title "Coney Island Criminals" opened October 11, 2013 and ran 22 performances. Directed by Dick Zigun. Designs by Kate Dale, Marie Roberts, Alix Martin. Recorded Music by Steven Kapplan. Cast: Scott Baker, Michael DiMinico, Amanda Jencsik, Elisa Marti, Luis Michaels and Adam Mick.

Revised and renamed The Education Of Al Capone As If Told By Jimmy Durante A Brooklyn Showcase Premiere opened November 2, 2018 and ran 5 previews and 10 performances at Sideshows By The Seashore in Brooklyn. Directed by Dick Zigun Scenery and Costumes by Kate Dale. Cast: Rob Aloi; Nikos Brisco; Natalie Michaels; Rita Posillico; Rob Romeo; and Will Thomas.

CAST OF HISTORICAL CHARACTERS

JIMMY DURANTE - A timeless entertainer, a middle-aged star of stage and screen, remembering the early days Italian, straw hat.

FRANKIE YALE - Dapper Brooklyn Gangster in his 30's, Italian, raccoon coat, pork-pie hat

AL CAPONE - 18 years old, Italian, black derby, black vest, red Union shirt

CLARA BOW - 14-year-old waitress dreaming of Hollywood Stardom, Irish Redhead, Betty Boop prototype.

FRANK GALLUCIO, etc. Male characters, Italian, quick change artist.

LENA GALLUCIO, etc. Female characters, in her twenties Italian, quick change artist.

TIME

1917

PLACE

THE HARVARD INN - A Coney Island Saloon on The Bowery behind Nathan's.

PRODUCTION NOTES

Advertisements for the show should include the motto- "Warm Beer. Lousy Pasta. $5"

The Lobby of the Theatre should have a sign which reads:

Patrons are advised that these performances will include:

Cigar Smoking

Blank Gun Fire

Profanity

Anachronisms

Ethnic Stereotypes

Sexual Situations

Dramatic License

and Ballistic Pasta

Some of the audience sits front and center at cabaret tables and chairs. To one side is a Bar, piano and entrance door. The room is painted Harvard crimson and decorated with sarcastic Harvard memorabilia. On the other side of the audience is the exterior of Frankie Yale's private office painted in Yale blue and decorated in sarcastic Yale memorabilia featuring a "Skull & Bones Secret Society" sign hanging over a locked closet door.

This play is a Dirty Dinner Theater Brechtian Cabaret. It is an immersive interactive production, Tony and Tina's Wedding meets avantgarde performance art. There is no Fourth Wall.

Big budget productions will include a full piece jazz band; budget productions should at least have one or two pianists.

SCENE ONE

(JIMMY DURANTE enters for work and warms up at the piano. He ad libs small talk and jokes with the audience and then the house lights dim.)

DURANTE

I once knew a girl so dumb. How Dumb? So dumb they had to burn down the schoolhouse to get her out of the third grade. I got a million of 'em.

(Ad libs. Jokes. One-liners. Warm up the Audience. Finally)

My pal Eddie Cantor just taught me this song.

(He plays THE DUMBER THEY COME THE BETTER I LIKE EM, 1923 Public Domain by Stephen DeRosa.)

I may look simple but I want you to know
I've been to college, I'm full of knowledge
I'm right at home with brainy men and then, my wisdom I show
But when there's clever girls around I get up and go

Those educated babies are a bore
I'm gonna say what I said many times before
Oh, the dumber they come, the better I like 'em
'Cause the dumb ones know how to make love

A wisenheimer has you meet her folks when you call
The brainless baby always keeps you down in the hall
Oh, the dumbbells I've met, have won beauty prizes
They look like angels sent from above

The clever girl will want to know if you mean to wed
The dumb ones never think of looking that far ahead
That's why the dumber they come, the better I like 'em

'Cause the dumb ones know how to make love

Oh, the dumber they come, the better I like 'em
'Cause the dumb ones know how to make love

DURANTE

Inka Dinka Do

That's What I Do

From Me To You

Folks, it's Showtime! Allow myself to introduce myself, I'm Jimmy Durante, your Host for the next ninety minutes and my advice is: the more you drink, the better the show! Do tip your waitress, bartender, and piano player, if we please you, and if you ain't pleased, keep your big mouth shut... dems the rules. Feel free to smoke cigars, get drunk, and if you gotta spit on the floor, please use a spittoon, as dis is a respectable saloon.

I'm feeling awful nostalgic tonight...something about this room...the tin ceiling...the old bar...re minds me of my first job...before Prohibition...what a Summer...young Ragtime Jimmy appearing nightly at a Jazz Joint by the beach, a joint at Coney Island called Harvard Inn...The Harvard Inn was gangster Frankie Yale's place... Harvard...Yale...Get it? You gotta have a Coney Island sense of humor... it's Shtick! Thick Shtick! Where was I? We was way backwards in me memory...My first job...Harvard Inn...Al Capone's first job...Clara Bow's first job...True Story...almost...the way I remember...

(He goes back to piano plays a few chords.)

Inka Dinka Do

That's What I Do

From Me To You

(Lights out on DURANTE. A BARTENDER and WAITRESS enter as DURANTE sits with Audience.)

Every half hour I get a break and the Staff of The Harvard Inn puts on a Floor Show!

SCENE TWO

(BARTENDER and WAITRESS don Harvard aprons, raise mugs of beer and sing the "Harvard University Fight Song", 1918 Public Domain by A. Putnam)

WAITRESS

Ten thousand men of Harvard

Want vict'ry today.

BARTENDER (Off-Key)

Ten thousand men of Harvard

Want vict'ry today.

WAITRESS

For they know that o'er old Eli

Fair Harvard holds sway.

BARTENDER

For they know that o'er old Eli

Fair Harvard holds sway.

WAITRESS AND BARTENDER

So then we'll conquer old Eli's men,

And when the game ends, we'll sing again;

Ten thousand men of Harvard

Gained vict'ry today!

DURANTE (Aside)

I didn't say it was a GOOD floor show...Drinks is on the house!

(aside)

That is if you're seated in the front row...

(BARTENDER and WAITRESS work tables, serve drinks.)

SCENE THREE

(ORCHESTRA/PIANIST CUE: in the style of the 1921 recording by The Original Dixieland Jazz Band: "Jazz Me Blues.")

(As music continues to play there is a 5 minute dance party scene...FRANKIE YALE wearing a Yale sweater and Raccoon Coat enters, shakes hands and passes out cigars to the audience from a cigar box with his dapper smiling face on the label. It is a major meet and greet opportunity for the audience to get to know FRANKIE YALE. In the background new strange unknown characters lurk in the shadows. ...AL CAPONE enters and moves like an escaped convict hugging the prison wall to avoid the spotlight, sometimes spitting sometimes scratching his balls...CLARA BOW hardly enters, rather she peeks her head in from various hiding spots. Music out.)

(BLACKOUT)

SCENE FOUR

(BARTENDER & WAITRESS snatch free beers from the hands and tables of the audience.)

DURANTE

Management suggests you folks pay for this second round of drinks or give up your front row good seats to paying customers.

(Some audience members are forced to change seats.)

And now my story continues without further commercial interruption... at least, that is, until we move you two when and if more VIPS show up...so one day that Summer some tough Italian teenage hoodlum, some son of a bad Brooklyn barber...some tough, teenage thug in a black Derby and black vest dressed like some matinee bad guy just burst through the door!

(AL CAPONE bursts through the door. He goes up to the bar.)

AL CAPONE

I'm here to talk to the boss.

BARTENDER

Boss ain't here. You got an appointment?

AL CAPONE

Then I'll wait.

WAITRESS

You can't just wait...you gotta order something from the menu.

(She pushes CAPONE down in a chair at a table. She puts a menu in his face. CAPONE rips up the menu as he speaks.)

AL CAPONE

Bring me a big bowl of Spaghetti...WAIT...not Spaghetti and Meatballs, just Spaghetti. WAIT.... not Spaghetti with red or white sauce, just Spaghetti...WAIT...not Spaghetti. Bring me a big bowl of hot Linguini...and bring me grated cheese and a beer...and bring me two big forks...and two big knives...and bring it to me NOW!

WAITRESS

Plate of plain Spaghetti coming right up!

DURANTE

This kid who wanted to talk to the boss was wild like an animal! I'm gonna go over and sit in with the band. Let's serenade the kid while he eats with a tune I call: "Bow Wow Blues..."

(DURANTE exits to the bar. ORCHESTRA/PIANIST CUE: in the style of the 1921 recording by The Original Dixieland Jazz Band: "Bow Wow Blues". Everyone barks like a dog and makes animal sounds.)

(WAITRESS serves AL CAPONE a big bowl of Spaghetti, 2 knives and 2 forks. CAPONE makes a big deal out of sharpening the knives, cuts the spaghetti, stabs knives into table, stabs forks into table, takes out and opens switchblade knife, puts on brass knuckles, and uses those weapons as utensils to eat spaghetti like an animal...AUDIENCE FEELS strands of wet spaghetti land on their h eads.)

(Song ends...eating ends...)

WAITRESS

The Boss, Mr. Yale, is in now. Whom shall I say is calling? Mr...?

AL CAPONE

Capone is my name.

(CAPONE shoves spaghetti in her face.)

WILL THOMAE as teenage Alfonso Capone eating spaghetti. Photo by Norman Blake.

WILL THOMAE as teenage Alfonso Capone starting a food fight with the audience. Photo by Norman Blake.

SCENE FIVE

(OUTSIDE THE OFFICE DOOR: CAPONE knocks, a different door opens.)

FRANKIE YALE

What do you want kid?

AL CAPONE

I want a job

FRANKIE YALE

Do you know who I am?

AL CAPONE

Frankie Yale. You're a cold-hearted blood-thirsty killer...and I mean that as a compliment...you own this place, you own lots of things...I want to learn how to own things...

FRANKIE YALE

You don't have enough class to own things. Any things.

AL CAPONE

Me? If I don't have class then I'll buys class! If I can't afford class, I'll steals class. You should gives me a job.

FRANKIE YALE

You can have one of my cigars.

AL CAPONE

That's a start...Hey, that's you on the label!

FRANKIE YALE

It's called a cigar band. And that is me on top of the box! I'm on top!

(They light cigars. Smoke Cigars. It turns into a lengthy cigar-smoking contest. Here and there the following lines intersperse with mad puffing.)

AL CAPONE

Why are we standing *outside* of your office?

(Smoking pause.)

FRANKIE YALE

That ain't my office, this door here, that's my office. The sign on that door says "Keep Out- Skull & Bones". (Smoking pause.)

AL CAPONE

What's Skull & Bones?

FRANKIE YALE

Skull & Bones is a Yale Secret Society.

AL CAPONE

What's that mean, Secret Society? (Smoking pause.)

FRANKIE YALE

(Whispering:)

How do-you-a-say Skull & Bones in Italian? It's the Black Hand, you Coney Island idiot, and we can't let you inside the meeting room unless you're a made member: STAY OUTSIDE! Capisce? (Smoking pause)

AL CAPONE

You run everything in Brooklyn, you should make me a member.

FRANKIE YALE

Murdering somebody is a prerequisite for membership...you ever murder anyone, Baby Face?

(CAPONE intentionally bumps into YALE.)

BARTENDER (Aside)

This shit just got real.

SCENE SIX

(FRANKIE YALE & AL CAPONE perform a choreographed boxing match. DURANTE has a bell and hammer to indicate match rounds. CAPONE boxes like a street brawler...YALE boxes formal-old-school-collegiate style. DURANTE strikes the bell.)

DURANTE

It's Fight Night on the inside, Folks...dis is why we ain't got nice things...

ROUND ONE

Although it wasn't his fault

Capone got too close

Stumbled and pushed Yale off the asphalt

So Yale ups to Capone

And Capone ups to Yale

Capone says, it wasn't his fault

WILL THOMAE as Al Capone boxes NIKOS BRISCO as Frankie Yale. Photo by Norman Blake.

CAPONE (With Durante)

It wasn't my fault

DURANTE

Yale swings and yells back, sure wasn't his fault

YALE (With Durante)

Sure wasn't my fault

DURANTE

Capone says, I said it was an accident

It wasn’t my fault

CAPONE (With DURANTE)

It was an accident

DURANTE

Yale swings again

And yells again, it sure is your fault

YALE (With DURANTE)

It sure is your fault

DURANTE

And Yale keeps yelling, if you don't like it, Baby Face

I'll punch you right in the proboscis

WILL THOMAE as Al Capone boxes NIKOS BRISCO as Frankie Yale with ROB ROMEO as Jimmy Durante refereeing the fight. Photo by Norman Blake.

YALE (With DURANTE)

If you don't like it, Baby Face

I'll punch you right in the proboscis

DURANTE

Punches him right in the nose

(FRANKIE YALE swings back and hits DURANTE on the nose. DURANTE strikes the bell, ending the round. FRANKIE YALE and AL CAPONE go to their corners.)

ROUND TWO

I even take a stray punch in the proboscis

(Never healed, obviously.)

I was so mad I was frosted at the kneecaps and hid under the piano

(CAPONE spits out a broken tooth.)

(DURANTE strikes the bell to start the next round.)

ROUND THREE

Capone ups to Yale, Yale ups to Capone

Yale ups to Capone again & again & again like a punching bag

(The fight and the dialogue switches to SLOW MOTION.)

But it don't do nothing to the kid, Capone doesn't go down

He just uses his attitude and wins us all over, even Yale

(DURANTE strikes the bell, ending the round. FRANKIE YALE and AL CAPONE go to their corners. DURANTE strikes the bell to start the next round.)

ROUND FOUR

And with that, to show the Boss who's Boss

Capone puts a chip on his shoulder

And says knock it off, Boss, anytime, knock it off

CAPONE (With DURANTE)

Knock it off, Boss, anytime, knock it off

DURANTE

Five minutes later the chip was still there but Capone's shoulder was gone

Yale slaps Capone in the face and says

If you ever betray or disobey me, I'll ups you again

And then I'll have my boys ups you some more

YALE (With DURANTE)

If you ever betray or disobey me, I'll ups you again

And then I'll have my boys ups you some more

DURANTE

Yale says, we do things here my way

And you'll do things my way or I'll knock you down

And pick you up and knock you down and pick you up

YALE (With DURANTE)

We do things here my way and you'll do things my way

Or I'll knock you down and pick you up

And knock you down and pick you up...

DURANTE

And Capone was smiling through it all, he had to smile

Frankie Yale had his fist in Capone's mouth!

(DURANTE rings his bell several times.)

Frankie Yale wins by a TKO. Frankie Yale, winner and still champion. Winner - Winner – Chicken Dinner.

(ORCHESTRA/PIANIST CUE: in the style of the 1918 recording by The Original Dixieland Jazz Band: "Skeleton Jangle".)

BLACKOUT

SCENE SEVEN

(Music out.)

(BARTENDER enters & removes coat & starts to set up bar. WAITRESS enters and removes coat & sets up tables. DURANTE enters & removes coat.)

DURANTE

Stop the music! Stop the music! Management would like the staff to listen to an important announcement before the Harvard Inn opens tonight:

(FRANKIE YALE enters with his arm around AL CAPONE.)

FRANKIE YALE

I want all you pisanos to meet our new Bartender, Alfonso Capone.

(Old BARTENDER clears his throat.)

Al, I want you to meet Eli, my Bulldog, my former Bartender and the Harvard Inn's new Dean of Bouncers. Al...Eli... Al, meet Columbia the Gem of Waitresses...and the *Schnozzola* over there is Ragtime Jimmy, Piano Player.

DURANTE (offering his hand)

Charmed, I'm sure.

AL CAPONE

So now that I've got the job, what is the job, boss?

FRANKIE YALE

You work here, you wear a uniform.

AL CAPONE

Whatever you say, Boss.

(ELI pulls a Harvard apron over CAPONE's head.)

ENTIRE CAST (SINGS:)

"Ten Thousand Men of Harvard," etc.

(YALE pulls the Harvard apron off CAPONE then flips it around, revealing a Yale apron which he puts over CAPONE's head.)

ENTIRE CAST

(SINGS:)

("YALE FIGHT SONG" public domain by Allan M. Hirsh, 1901.)

Bulldog! Bulldog!

Bow, Wow, Wow

Eli Yale!

Bulldog! Bulldog!

Bow, Wow, Wow

Our Team Can Never Fail!

(THEY force CAPONE to sing and dance.)

Boola-Boola!

Boola-Boola!

AL CAPONE

Stop the music, stop the fuckin' music.

DURANTE

Everybody's trying to get into my act, even Al Capone's stealing my act.

AL CAPONE

What else should I learn my first day of Freshman Orientation?

WAITRESS

(WAITRESS drops a pill in a glass.)

How to slip someone a Mickey.

BOUNCER

Today's Password is: "Princeton."

FRANKIE YALE

Don't ask questions about what happens in my office.

AL CAPONE

You mean over there, Skull and Bones?

FRANKIE YALE

Why you gotta ask questions? Eli doesn't ask questions. Eli, I want you to go into the Pavilion of Fun at Steeplechase Amusement Park and stare at yourself in the Fun House Mirrors and make funny faces for four hours. Do it!

BOUNCER

Yes, Boss.

(BOUNCER leaves making funny faces as he exits through the audience. ORCHESTRA/PIANIST CUE: in the style of the 1921 recording by The Original Dixieland Jazz Band: "St. Louis Blues".)

SCENE EIGHT

(Same actor who plays BARTENDER now re-enters as COP.)

AL CAPONE

Welcome to the Harvard Inn. Private Club. Do you know the-

COP

The password is "Princeton". Never seen you before. You must be Yale's brand new pledge, but you're not one of us... yet.

AL CAPONE

What are you drinking?

WAITRESS

What are you eating?

DURANTE

Got any requests?

COP

Sing me the Whiffenpoof Song. All of you. (To Audience) ALL OF YOUSE.

CAST & AUDIENCE

(Whiffenpoof Song public domain 1909 by Galloway/Minnigerode/Pomeroy)

We're poor little lambs

Who've lost our way

Baa, baa, baa

We're little black sheep

Who've gone astray

Baa, baa, baa

Gentlemen songsters off on a spree

Doomed from here to eternity

Lord have mercy on such as we

Baa, baa, baa

(Repeat song with bouncing ball visuals.)

We're poor little lambs

Who've lost our way

Baa, baa, baa

We're little black sheep

Who've gone astray

Baa, baa, baa

Gentlemen songsters off on a spree

Doomed from here to eternity

Lord have mercy on such as we

Baa, baa, baa

SCENE NINE

(As others sing FRANKIE YALE and COP evict audience from a private table and move the table to a private location. They sit and divide money.)

FRANKIE YALE

I love show business!

COP

You love every business where you're the boss, Frankie: Saloon Business. Ice Delivery Business. Protection Business. Funeral Parlor Business. Cigar Factory Business.

FRANKIE YALE

It's all business! Have a cigar!

COP

Who's the Freshman, Frankie?

FRANKIE YALE

You mean my new Bartender?

(Whistles loudly.)

Baby Face?

(CAPONE enters.)

AL CAPONE

My name is Capone, A-L-F-O-N-S-O Capone.

COP

You got a record, Baby Face?

AL CAPONE

No, Sir.

(The entire cast, except CAPONE, laugh. The entire cast, except CAPONE, exit.)

No, Sir...I don't have a Rap Sheet...not yet, Sir... after work I'm going back to the Shooting Gallery...I need to practice shooting a gun...sir. Off-i-seur, I like the authoritarian example you set, Sir, Officer... and I mean that as a compliment.

(CAPONE goes to an arcade Shooting Gallery game and practices) (ORCHESTRA/PIANIST CUE: in the style of the 1921 recording by The Original Dixieland Jazz Band: "Margie".)

(BLACKOUT)

SCENE TEN

(Music out. The door opens. For a brief moment, sunshine spills into the dive bar. Sound Cue: Seagulls and Ocean.)

CLARA BOW

I'm looking for Mr. Durante. Hello? I'm looking for Mr. Durante? Hello?

DURANTE

Dats me! What a coincidence who are you, Kewpie Doll?

CLARA BOW

I'm a friend of your friend, Nathan Handwerker, from Nathan's Hot Dogs, around the corner.. .here in Coney...I cook the corn on the cob at the counter...for the customers...boopdedoop!

DURANTE

Boopdedoop? Oh, I've heard all about you, Kewpie Doll...you're Nathan's underage Bun Slicer, right?

CLARA BOW

Not anymore I'm not...Ida, Mrs. Handwerker, caught Nathan, Mr. Handwerker...pinching my Buns...while he was hand-jerking-working his hotdog...boopdedoop! Nathan said you owe him a favor and I could ask...you...for...a job right here!

(CLARA grabs DURANTE's crotch.)

DURANTE

Boopdedoop what's your name, Kewpie Doll?

CLARA BOW

Clara Bow...I need a new job waitressing...but I wanna be an actress!

DURANTE

I'm thinking she could bring us the Irish clientele...the sex offender clientele...and at the moment I owe some money to Nathan, so as long as the Boss approves, for the rest of the summer I got a new sidekick!

CLARA BOW

BoopDeBoop!

DURANTE

Let me go talk to the boss.

CLARA BOW

Let me do the talking, silly. BoopDeDoop!

(BLACKOUT)

SCENE ELEVEN

(LIGHTS UP on full staff with FRANKIE YALE.)

FRANKIE YALE

I want all of you pisanos to meet our new waitress, Clara Bow just matriculated to Harvard from Sheepshead Bay School of Hard Knocks.

(BLACKOUT)

SCENE TWELVE

(LIGHTS UP on CLARA BOW sitting on FRANKIE YALE's lap.)

You work here...you wear a uniform...

CLARA BOW

(CLARA BOW lets her dress fall to the floor.)

Whatever you say, Boss...

(ORCHESTRA/PIANIST CUE: in the style of the 1918 recording by TheOriginal Dixieland Jazz Band: "Bluin' The Blues".)

(BLACKOUT)

SCENE THIRTEEN

(Music out.)

(MAN IN AUDIENCE sneaks into place and sits at a table. CAPONE poses at the Shooting Gallery trying out several guns: rifle, pistol, sub-machine gun.)

FRANKIE YALE

Fellow Men of Harvard, won't you make some noise for our feature headliner Ragtime Jimmy! And introducing the BoopDeDoop Girl, Clara Bow.

(DURANTE & BOW sing a parody with new lyrics to the tune of: "Did You Ever Have The Feeling?")

DURANTE

Every once and awhile even a nice guy like me ends up contemplating bloody murder...

Did you ever have the feeling

That you wanted to kill

But still had the feeling

That you wanted to play

You know what's right not doing wrong

Still wrong will be here ‘fore too long

DURANTE AND CLARA

It's tough to have the feeling

That you want to kill

And still have the feeling

That you want to play

Urge to kill

Change your mind

Urge to kill again but

Change your mind again

It's tough to have the feeling

That you want to kill

And still have the feeling

That you want to play

Eenie Meenie Miney Moe, Catch a victim by the toe:

I kill I will

DURANTE (ad libs as CLARA sings)

You're killing it...Knock 'em dead...slay 'em...if you got it, gal, kill 'em with it...

(AL CAPONE grabs a MAN IN AUDIENCE sticks a gun in his gut and fires a "real" gun, with blanks, to kill for the first time...AUDIENCE FEELS water-spray splatter via WAITRESS squirting a water pistol in the dark)

(ORCHESTRA/PIANIST CUE: in the style of the 1917 recording by The Original Dixieland Jazz Band: "Crazy Blues". CAPONE sprays bullets over the heads of remaining live audience patrons.)

(BLACKOUT and Music out)

SCENE FOURTEEN

(LIGHTS UP on FRANKIE YALE.)

FRANKIE YALE

I want all you pisanos to meet the Harvard Inn's new Dean of Bouncers, Alfonso Capone, now to be known as Crazy Face, growing up fast in my world...come over here, Crazy Face...

(They sit at his desk)

Just prick your finger with this Phi Beta Capa pin for some blood...just smear your blood on this picture of Cole Porter...just keep holding this stick of TNT while it burns in your hand..BOOM!

(He snuffs out the TNT fuse)

Such a good student! Come talk to me inside "Skull and Bones"...Clara? You come inside too...B oopDeDoop!

AL CAPONE

Clara's no made member!

FRANKIE YALE

I was gonna give her to you, in honor of popping your cherry...first kill followed by a fine fuck...rites of passage...

(Tracer Light illuminate the Skull & Bones sign)

(FRANKIE YALE whistles and blindfolds AL CAPONE and CLARA BOW who follows him inside "Skull and Bones". He places CLARA's hand on CAPONE's shoulder and then YALE places CAPONE's hand on his own shoulder. He leads them, blindfolded through the audience and finally they exit into Skull & Bones. The door slams shut. Laughter from within. DURANTE bangs on the door.)

DURANTE

Clara! Clara!

(DURANTE sings "G'wan Home, Your Mudder's Callin" by Fain/Freed© 1947. If rights cannot be secured another song in the same style should be substituted.)

(First Song Verse)

(Office door opens CLARA stands in the door blocking DURANTE.)

CLARA BOW

I'll fuck the entire football team if I feel like it!

(Door slams shut on DURANTE'S nose.)

DURANTE

(Song Chorus)

(Second Verse)

(Office door opens CAPONE stands in the door, pants down around his ankles, blocking DURANTE.)

AL CAPONE

(Chorus)

You've got the biggest nose I've ever seen, Durante...it's even bigger than my big balls...and I mean that as a compliment!

(Door slams shut on DURANTE's nose.)

DURANTE

If they won't let me in there...maybe I'm the one who should go home...

(The tracer lights on the sign turn off. DURANTE puts on his hat and coat. He wanders into the audience and finishes the song sitting on someone's lap.)

(Chorus)

(DURANTE cries, blows his nose into a handkerchief and exits.)

(BLACKOUT)

SCENE FIFTEEN

DURANTE

Night after night, all summer long: We worked together...we schlepped together... we slept toget her...I even got a bit of "BoopDeDoop"'s ass...in my defense there wasn't no Mrs. Calabash yet at that time.

CLARA BOW

I even got to sing on stage with Jimmy Durante. He taught me lots of things about showbiz on stage and off stage. I sat on his lap while we both put on makeup...I wasn't a Hollywood movie star yet at that time.

AL CAPONE

I even got some Executive experience running various shady things in Coney Island...I wasn't a successful Chicago businessman yet at that time.

FRANKIE YALE

You want to know what time it is, pisanos? It's time to open for business tonight. Get to work!

SCENE SIXTEEN

(TWO HIGH-CLASS CUSTOMERS knock on the door.)

AL CAPONE

Welcome to the Harvard Inn. Members Only. What's the password?

CUSTOMERS

Dartmouth.

FRANKIE YALE

Welcome, customers! What are you drinking?

CLARA BOW

What are you eating?

DURANTE

Got any requests? Sure we know that one!

(DURANTE & CLARA BOW sing a parody of the tune of: "Little Bit This, Little Bit That, Everybody Knows My Gal." with new lyrics.)

DURANTE

I'm gonna tell you bout a gal that's got it

I'm gonna tell you bout a doll so cute

When I tell you bout the girl that's got it

BoopDeDoop

BoopDeDoop

BoopDeDoop

CLARA

I've got it and I've got that

I'm a little bit this and a little bit that

And a little bit short and a little bit fat

DURANTE

It seems everybody loves this gal

CLARA

I'm a little bit short and a little bit BoopDeDoop

DURANTE

It seems everybody loves this gal

CLARA

No wonder they love me my nose turns up

DURANTE

My nose turns down and every time we kiss we lock bumpers! Hey, Clara. You wanna play bumping cars with me?

(CLARA screams and shakes and slaps the TWO HIGH-CLASS CUSTOMERS.)

CLARA BOW

Don't kiss me, Durante! Everybody keep your hands off me! Mommy! Mommy!

My crazy mother held a knife to my throat while I was dreaming in bed...I THOUGHT I woke up but nothing changed... I'm so scared I'm awake in a nightmare, my mother saying, "Clara you'd be better off dead than an actress!"...last night my crazy mother put a sharp knife to my throat! Why do I have to get pawed to get ahead?

(CUSTOMERS flee. BLACKOUT.)

SCENE SEVENTEEN

(ORCHESTRA/PIANIST CUE: in the style of the 1918 recording by The Original Dixieland Jazz Band: "At the Jazz Band Ball".)

(Music out. Two nervous MIDDLE-CLASS CUSTOMERS knock at the door.)

AL CAPONE

Welcome to the Harvard Inn. Private Club. What's the password?

TWO NEW CUSTOMERS

Brown University?

FRANKIE YALE

Welcome, Customers! What are you drinking?

CLARA BOW

What are you eating?

DURANTE

Got any requests? Sure, we know that!

(DURANTE plays two chords on the piano.)

(YALE breaks a pool cue over the heads of TWO MIDDLE-CLASS CUSTOMERS and throws billiard balls and beer bottles after them as they flee. BLACKOUT)

SCENE EIGHTEEN

(ORCHESTRA/PIANIST CUE: in the style of the 1918 recording by The Original Dixieland Jazz Band: "At the Jazz Band Ball".)

(Music out. TWO LOW-CLASS CUSTOMERS knock at the door. The Man dressed in drag and the Woman wearing a fake mustache that falls off.)

AL CAPONE

Welcome to the Harvard Inn. Private Club. What's the password?

TWO NEWER CUSTOMERS

University of Pennsylvania? Um... No, no...maybe? Wait a minute, I'm with it, I swear. I think Cornell is the password today?

CAPONE

This way to Ithaca...

(CAPONE leads the Man in drag off-stage & shoots and kills the "CORNELL" CUSTOMER.)

FRANKIE YALE (To traumatized Woman customer)

Welcome, Customer. What are you drinking?

CLARA BOW

What are you eating?

DURANTE

I'm not taking requests. I'm taking my break.

(CLARA BOW sings "Harvard Fight Song" sitting on NEWEST CUSTOMER's lap.)

(BLACKOUT)

SCENE NINETEEN

(AL CAPONE sings "Harvard Fight Song" gazing at his image in a mirror while combing and re-combing and re-re-combing his hair. He breaks the mirror. BLACKOUT.)

(ORCHESTRA/PIANIST CUE: in the style of the 1919 recording by The Original Dixieland Jazz Band: "Fidgety Feet".)

(Video FLASH FORWARD TO FILM CLIP OF St. Valentine's Day Massacre. Lots of men killed via tommy guns. AUDIENCE FEELS and hears lots and lots of gunshots in the dark. Gunshots and flashes from different directions.)

DURANTE

Stop the music!

(Music out.)

It's a catastastastroke! A bloody catastrophe! Management says dis situation is serious!

FRANKIE YALE

I want all yous to understand I lost too many Secret Society members last night...I want all of my pisanos to go out and round up every prospect you can find in Coney Island tonight...bring me everyone you've had your eyes on...find me prospects, find me soldiers...but keep this discrete, just go up and tap em on the shoulder...whisper in their ear...Frankie Yale wants to see you at Skull and Bones right away...

INTERMISSION

(ORCHESTRA/PIANIST CUE: in the style of the 1917 recording by The Original Dixieland Jazz Band: "Dixie Jass Band One-Step")

(During this 15 Minute Intermission patrons may go to the bathroom, they can buy drinks at the bar, however, One by one, ALL AUDIENCE MEMBERS experience: being tapped on the shoulder by DURANTE or being picked up and dragged by AL CAPONE into Skull and Bones, a black-light-lit corridor or a dark closet with no lighting; FRANKIE YALE might pour water into their hands; YALE might simulate having their finger bitten by a human skull's jaw or tapped on the head with a human thigh bone as ceremoniously manipulated by FRANKIE YALE as he shouts a Rule or Threat per audience member...loud enough for the entire audience to hear.)

SAMPLE RULES

Rule #1 The only good rat is a dead rat!

Rule #2 You see something, you don't say nothing!

Rule #3 Don't talk to the cops unless the cop's with me!

or

I NEED SOLDIERS. Hey it's just you and me alone for your Skull and Bones initiation. You have a choice: (1) stick your dick into the mouth of this skull and scream "Geronimo" cause it's Geronimo's skull; (2) stick this leg bone up your asshole as you scream "Please General Custard, I don't wanna go", as it's actually Custard's leg bone...

Once everyone has experienced Skull and Bones and gone to the bathroom, lights out.

ACT TWO

SCENE TWENTY

FRANKIE YALE (as Intermission Ends)

YOU can kiss my ring, YOU can kiss my cheek, and YOU can kiss my ass... Maybe I give YOU a Yale scholarship, a good grade point average, some Yale mafia connections. Now that YOU'RE a made member of Skull and Bones YOU'RE above the law- YOU can lie, YOU can steal, YOU can kill, YOU can grab women but nobody can touch YOU. No means yes, yes means anal. YOU go to Harvard or Yale consider YOURSELF privileged, consider YOURSELF rich and entitled. YOU can start out doing gardening work. Grow me some ivy on those walls over there!

FRANKIE YALE

If you don't like men like me...just keep out of our way...or "Ba Fungul"...we run things. Kiss my varsity ring or my Hand points its finger at you! Hey, Ba Fungul!

(He slams the door shut. Another door opens and CLARA BOW stands in front of it. She gargles and spits a gross amount of goo into a spittoon.)

CLARA BOW

BoopDeDoop.

(She lights a cigar.)

If you don't like women like me...just keep out of our way...or "Fungul"...I'm learning Italian...yo ung women give the finger to you, Mister! Hey, Ba Fungul! My Irish white hand gives the finger to all of you!

SCENE TWENTY ONE

(She slams her door shut. AL CAPONE enters and knocks on YALE's door.)

AL CAPONE (pointing at audience.)

You know, Boss you gave those there Coney Island Collegiate Kids a nice set of rules...

(Knocks again.)

...and I mean that as a compliment...

(Knocks again.)

...but what's next for me, Boss?

(The door opens.)

FRANKIE YALE

Harvard Inn opens in five minutes, pisanos! Let's get back to work!

(BLACKOUT)

SCENE TWENTY TWO

(FRANK and LENA GALLUCIO enter.)

AL CAPONE

Welcome to the Harvard Inn.

(He whistles as she walks.)

Honey, with curves like that you don't need any password.

(He allows LENA to pass but blocks FRANK.)

FRANK GALLUCIO

The password is Boystown Reform School for Retarded Juvenile Delinquent Orphans.

(CAPONE pulls out a stool for LENA, watches her sit and whistles.)

I'm drinking hard whiskey, leave the bottle...and the LADY here just wants an Egg Cream.

LENA GALLUCIO

Grazie.

(AL CAPONE makes an Egg Cream and hands it to LENA GALLUCIO.)

AL CAPONE

Bottoms up, Honey.

(He whistles. CLARA BOW gets between CAPONE and LENA.)

CLARA BOW

What are you eating?

AL CAPONE

I know what I'm eating fifteen minutes from now.

FRANK GALLUCIO

What's eating that guy?

(DURANTE gets between CAPONE and FRANK GALLUCIO.)

DURANTE

Got any requests, folks?

LENA GALLUCIO

Yes, I do have a request can you please ask that asshole to stop starring at my culo...it's embarrassi ng...

CLARA BOW & DURANTE

Al! Cut it out, Al.

LENA GALLUCIO

Frank, please ask him to stop it.

AL CAPONE

Honey, you got a nice ass and I mean that as a compliment, believe me.

(FRANK stands and faces CAPONE.)

LENA GALLUCIO

Ma come si permette? Avanti Frankie devi difendermi e difendere l'onore della famiglia.

FRANK GALLUCIO

I won't take this shit from nobody, so you better apologize immediately to my sister, LENA, or else!

LENA GALLUCIO

Esatto fatti valere!

AL CAPONE

Come on, Buddy, I'm only joking...no hard feelings...let me buy you something stiff, Lena, honey...

FRANK GALLUCIO

This is no fucking joke! I'm Frank Gallucio! I'm with Frankie Yale! I don't have to take this shit! My sister, Lena Gallucio, doesn't have to put up with this shit!

LENA GALLUCIO

Io non devo subire le insolenze di questo stronzo.

(CAPONE stops smirking at LENA and lunges at FRANK GALLUCIO. They fight, they hold each other, they knock things over. They fight in the audience. FRANK GALLUCIO and AL CAPONE each get hits on each other's bodies. FRANK GALLUCIO eventually pins AL CAPONE against the piano. FRANK GALLUCIO delivers three vicious kicks, each accompanied by hits on the piano keys, to put down AL CAPONE. AL CAPONE laughs as FRANK GALLUCIO pulls out a pocket knife. Three times he slashes at AL CAPONE but misses his throat. Instead, he slashes AL CAPONE's face three times. He yells as he slashes.)

FRANK GALLUCIO

I got you. Keep still so I can cut you and kill you. Stop squirming, kid. As soon as I get my pocketknife open you're history. I'm trying to SLIT! YOUR! THROAT!

(Blood squirts from AL CAPONE's left cheek and squirts all over the AUDIENCE.)

LENA GALLUCIO

Cosi' Frankie, bene. Tagliagli la gola. BRAVO!

(BLACKOUT)

ROB ALOI as Frank Gallucio cuts WILL THOMAE's face as Al Capone. Photo by Norman Blake.

SCENE TWENTY THREE

DURANTE

(Tune of "St. James Infirmary." Traditional public domain. New lyrics)

It went down in the Bar Room

On the Bowery near the Beach

The Regulars were Drinking

And the whores were eating Peach

Capone was knocked out on the floor

His face was squirting red

I turned and faced the Audience

And this is what I said:

Stop the music! Hey, Rube! Al Capone is in trouble! Hey, Rube! Dat's my boy...somebody call an ambulance!

(CLARA BOW enters dressed as 1ST NURSE, and there is a 2nd NURSE. A DOCTOR also enters with an enormous sewing needle and yards of thread and scissors. They sew 30 stitches on the left side of CAPONE's face, from throat to ear. They are the CHORUS.)

Al went down to

CI Infirmary

He saw the surgeon there

Surgeon stitched Al's face on the operating table

30 stitches from his throat to his ear

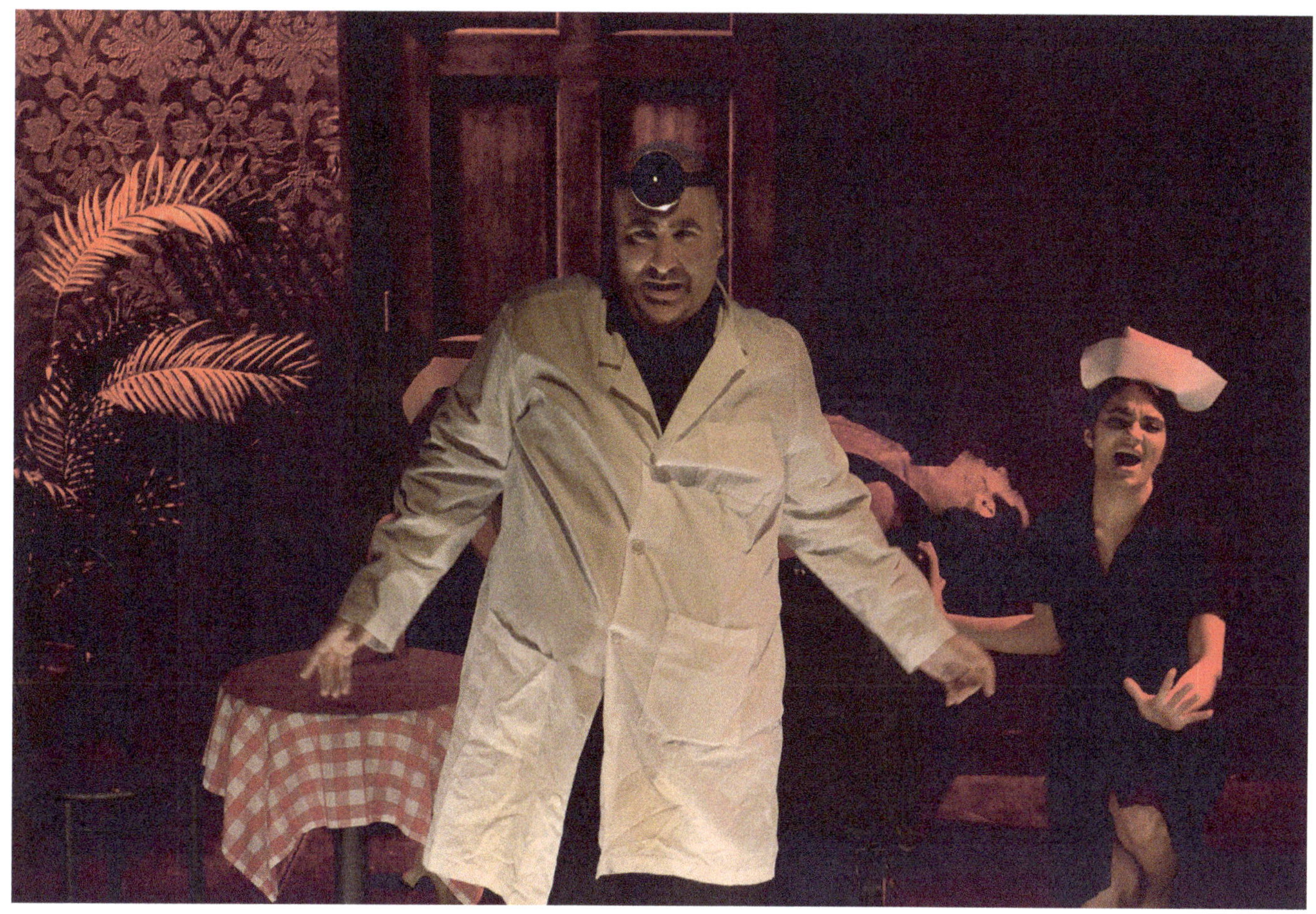

ROB ALOI as the Surgeon and RITA POSILLICO as the Nurse about to stitch up Capone's face. Photo by Norman Blake

DOCTOR

Let me sew! Let me stitch! I'm your Surgeon

CHORUS

Whoever you may be

Public Enemy #1 for all we care

DOCTOR

You'll never find a surgeon better than me

NURSES

Don't let him die!

DOCTOR

Let me sew!

NURSES

Don’t let him die!

DOCTOR

Let me sew!

CAPONE

Oh woe! Oh whoa!

CHORUS

Whoa! a horror show of slashes

The doctor did his best.

The CI infirmary was a bloody crazy mess.

DURANTE

He needs 16 stitches for slash #2

A dozen for slash #3

Pinch the clamp, Tie the knot, Stick the needle in the flesh

I'm so glad it didn't happen to me

CHORUS

Now that Capone's face is together

His Doctor has a habit for booze

And when anyone asks: Did you save Al Capone?

Doctor gets the Notoriety Blues.

(CAST exits.)

(BLACKOUT)

SCENE TWENTY FOUR

FRANKIE YALE

What a happy day today is, pisanos...the Harvard Inn's Head Bouncer is out of the hospital and back at Harvard to break heads...a round of applause, please, to welcome back my right hand man, Al Capone, to be now referred to as "Scarface." Scarface! Scarface! Scarface!

(EVERYONE applauds and yells, “Scarface!”)

AL CAPONE

(To Audience:)

Don't call me Scarface...you think that's a compliment?

FRANKIE YALE

Scars....tattoos...a crooked nose make a man look tough, and yes, I do mean that as a complimen t...Scars earn you respect...Scarface. Scarface! Scarface! Scarface!

DURANTE

Dats my boy!

AL CAPONE

Don't call me Scarface, FONGUL! I'm leaving! What did I learn at Harvard? Fuggedabout Brooklyn! It’s yours! I’m gonna become my own big bossman, boss. Fuggedaboutit! Chicago or Bust!

(AL CAPONE takes out a suitcase from behind the bar and starts packing.)

FRANKIE YALE

Clara Bow, come here, BoopDeDoop Girl. Go and round me up some new men.

CLARA BOW

Not me, Frankie, Darling...what I learned at Harvard is- the more I see of men...the more I like dogs...Hollywood or Bust.

(She starts packing a suitcase.)

Once I'm a Movie Star, I'll have my publicist edit my bio and not mention I worked anywhere else in Coney Island but Nathan's.

FRANKIE YALE

Jimmy Durante, come have a sit down with me maybe I can make you an offer that doubles your salary?

DURANTE

I got nuthin' but compliments to say about you, Boss, since the characters you meet on the way up are often the same creditors you meets on the way down...Broadway or bust.

(DURANTE Starts packing a suitcase.)

But I'm not fit for the life of a Coney Island Criminal...that's the little I learned at Harvard. Just imagine how easy it would be to spot my nose in a line up...I'll ask MY publicist to say MY first job was at the College Inn, which has no bad reputation, since it didn't exist! I'm off to find and marry Mrs. Calabash in Manhattan...or Hoboken, or wherever she is...meanwhile let's catch the next train out of town, Miss BoopDeDoop...

CLARA BOW

Do all men think about all day is whether I have a nice ass, Jimmy? Do you?

DURANTE

Grr...

(AL CAPONE shakes YALE's hand and stands by the exit door with suitcase.)

FRANKIE YALE

Alfonso went to Chicago and totally took over that little town...took it for everything he could. Public Enemy #1 and I'm the one taught him everything he knows.

(CLARA BOW kisses YALE on cheek and stands by the exit door with suitcase.)

Clara clipped a coupon in Motion Picture Magazine and won the 1st Prize Trophy in a Beauty Contest and a screen test in Hollywood. I taught her to smile on the outside while she's crying on the inside. Such a great actress.

(DURANTE rubs noses with YALE and leads CLARA BOW and AL CAPONE out the exit, carrying suitcases.)

Durante went legit on Broadway and became a huge star. Dats my boy, Jimmy! He was a natural I didn't have to teach Durante nuthin' at all. But right now it's time to get back to work and make money at Harvard! Staff needs to get the Brass Spittoons polished and the Saloon ready for new customers!

(BLACKOUT)

SCENE TWENTY FIVE

(WAITRESS in coat and hat smoking a cigarette directly addresses the audience.)

ORIGINAL WAITRESS

January 24, 1925

I mailed a postcard to my old friend:

Hi, Clara Bow, Greetings from Coney Island. The Harvard Inn burned down today and Frankie Yale's gonna take care of business from the back room of his Funeral Parlor...where his customers ain't drinking or eating anything so I'm looking for work...if you remember me, maybe you need another Maid at your Hollywood Mansion?

Wish I was there,

Columbia, The Gem of Waitresses

(She exits with a suitcase. BARTENDER takes off his apron, puts on black vestiments and puts out a vase of flowers. He directly addresses the audience.)

ORIGINAL BARTENDER

July 1, 1928

I mailed a postcard to my old associate:

Dear Alfonso: Greetings from Coney Island. I just shot the old Boss, Frankie Yale

(He gets nervous YALE might hear him.)

Shhh...I just took out our old boss, Frankie Yale just like you told me to do,Mr. Capone... Boss. We took all of the flowers all of the limos and hearses from Yale's own Funeral Parlor to bury Frankie in style. Thirty-eight Cadillac cars just to carry the flowers. Hell of a funeral, and I made sure everyone knows you paid for it, Mr. Capone... and meant it as a huge compliment!

Wish I was wit youse back in Chicago,

Eli, The Bulldog Mortician

(He shoots FRANKIE YALE then exits with a suitcase. DURANTE runs back onto the stage.)

SCENE TWENTY SIX

DURANTE

That's all, folks, that's the story! You don't have to go home but you can't stay here certainly...we're clearing the room...this room...there's something about it reminds me of the old Harvard Inn...I got a nose for dese things...The old bar? Dat ain't it...The tin ceiling? I don't think so...sniff sniff...It's the smell...the smell of the room...this room stinks like dat one did! Ha-Cha-Cha-C haaaa...goodnights, folks!

(DURANTE exits, blackout, then: CURTAIN CALL)

(Song Parody to the tune of, "I Know Darn Well I Can Do Without Broadway..." by Jimmy Durante. New lyrics)

(The music starts. DURANTE leads the CAST back onstage for the song. It is a call and response.)

DURANTE

You know it makes no difference what I started out to say—

YALE (Waking from being dead)

What is it?

CHORUS

Why Not?

DURANTE

It's dat time to wrap things up tie a bow around our show and tell the folks in the U.S. of A. what I wish to convey—

CHORUS

What is it?

DURANTE

Now you know damn well I can do without Harvard—

CHORUS

But!

DURANTE

Can Harvard do without me?

CHORUS

No!

DURANTE

Folks, I want you to put your hands together for the incredible, high flying, quick changing, Gallucios!

WAITRESS & BARTENDER

Now you know damn well I can do without Yalies—

CHORUS

But!

WAITRESS & BARTENDER

Can Yalies do without me?

(WAITRESS & BARTENDER bow.)

CHORUS

No!

DURANTE

The beautiful, the talented, the incredibly underaged Clara Bow!

CLARA BOW

Now you know damn well I can do without Coney—

CHORUS

But!

CLARA BOW

Can Coney do without me?

(CLARA BOW bows.)

CHORUS

No!

DURANTE

Those tough guys, those all around rough guys, Frankie Yale and Al Capone!

FRANKIE YALE & AL CAPONE

Now you know damn well we can do without Harvard—

CHORUS

But!

FRANKIE YALE & AL CAPONE

Can Harvard do without us?

(FRANKIE YALE & AL CAPONE bow.)

CHORUS

No!

DURANTE

I don't know...maybe I'm drunk...but just maybe they're forgetting something?

CLARA BOW

Ladies and Gentlemen: Jimmy Durante!

DURANTE

Now you know damn well I can do without Yalies—

CHORUS

But!

DURANTE

Can Yalies do without me?

(DURANTE bows, and brings the CAST forward.)

CHORUS

No!

(DURANTE brings the CAST forward.)

CAST

So you know damn well WE can do without Coney—

But!

Can Coney do without me?

(CAST bows and/or final pose.)

(BLACKOUT.)

(ORCHESTRA/PIANIST CUE: in the style of the 1918 recording of The Original Dixieland Jazz Band: “Tiger Rag”.)

THE END

THE LIFEGUARD CHOIR THEME SONG

By Dick D. Zigun

Vintage postcard from Collection of The Author. Illustrated Postal Card & Novelty Co., N.Y. (1907)

PRODUCTION HISTORY

THE LIFEGUARD CHOIR THEME SONG was originally developed as a skit within a full-length evening of short one-act plays about American holidays titled RED LETTER DAYS. A Brooklyn Showcase Premiere opened November 7, 1986, and ran for 16 performances at Sideshows By The Seashore, Produced by Coney Island, USA, funded in part by the National Endowment for the Arts, NYS Council on the Arts and NYC Department of Cultural Affairs.

Directed by Costa Mantis

Sets and Costumes by Holly Jaffe and Peter Levine.

Lighting by Joseph Errante.

Cast: Christine Linkie, Sturges Warner, Catherine Anne Hayes, Andrew Craig, Katy Dierlam, Patti Chambers.

TIME

Summertime. Late 1940's.

CAST

4 Lifeguards of any Age, Ethnicity, Weight or Sex. To be sung Acapella.

Summertime's Coming and I Wanna Be A Lifeguard

(But) I'm Glad I Wasn't A Lifeguard

(Back) In Nineteen Forty Somethin'

(When) That Famous Tropical Heatwave

(Put) The Lifeguards to The Test

(When) The Beach Was Full of Millions

(And) The Lifeguards Got No Rest

It's May Day -- First of May

May Day in The Surf Today

May Day -- Splish!

May Day -— Splash!

Two Communists Have Cramps!

Two Communists A Drowning!

Help Us! Save us!

Stroke! Stroke! -- The Dead Man's Float!

Splish! Splash!

One of Them Sank In The Icy Blue Sea

(Back) In Nineteen Forty Somethin'

(When) That Famous Tropical Heatwave

(Put) The Lifeguards To The Test

(When) The Beach was Full of Millions

(And) The Lifeguards Got No Rest

It’s Memorial Day —- End of May

Memorial Day In The Surf Today

Memorial Day -- Splish!

Memorial Day -- Splash!

Three Unknown Sailors On Shore Leave!

Three Unknown Sailors A Drowning!

Help us! Save us!

Two Communists Have Cramps!

Stroke! Stroke! —- The Dead Man‘s Float!

Splish! Splash!

One of Each Sank In The Icy Blue Sea

(Back) In Nineteen Forty Somethin'

(When) That Famous Tropical Heatwave

(Put) The Lifeguards To The Test

(When) The Beach Was Full of Millions

(And) The Lifeguards Got No Rest

It's Flag Day -- Midst of June

Flag Day In The Surf Today

Flag Day -- Splish!

Flag Day -- Splash!

Four Boy Scouts In A Kayak!

Four Boy Scouts A Drowning!

Help Us! Save Us!

Three Unknown Sailors On Shore Leave!

Stroke! Stroke! —- The Dead Man‘s Float!

Two Communists Have Cramps!

Splish! Splash!

One of Each Sank In The Icy Blue Sea

(Back) In Nineteen Forty Somethin'

(When) That Famous Tropical Heatwave

(Put) The Lifeguards To The Test

(When) The Beach Was Full of Millions

(And) The Lifeguards Got No Rest

It‘s Independence Day -- Fourth of July

Independence Day in The Surf Today

Independence Day -- Splish!

Independence Day -- Splash!

Five Little League Teams In A Tug of War!

Five Little League Teams A Drowning!

Help Us! Save Us!

Four Boy Scouts In A Kayak!

Stroke! Stroke! -— The Dead Man's Float!

Three Unknown Sailors On Shore Leave!

Splish! Splash!

Two Communists Have Cramps!

One of Each Sank In The Icy Blue Sea

(Back) In Nineteen Forty Somethin'

(When) That Famous Tropical Heatwave

(Put) The Lifeguards To The Test

(When) The Beach was Full of Millions

(And) The Lifeguards Got No Rest

It‘s Dog Days -- August Afternoons

Dog Days In The Surf Today

Dog Days -— Splish!

Dog Days -— Splash!

Six Irish Setters with Sunstroke!

Six Irish Setters A Drowning!

Help Us! Save Us!

Five Little League Teams In A Tug of War!

Stroke! Stroke! -— The Dead Man's Float!

Four Boy Scouts In A Kayak!

Splish! Splash!

Three Unknown Sailors On Shore Leave!

Two Communists Have Cramps!

One of Each Sank In The Icy Blue Sea

(Back) In Nineteen Forty Somethin'

(When) That Famous Tropical Heatwave

(Put) The Lifeguards To The Test

(When) The Beach was Full of Millions

(And) The Lifeguards Got No Rest

It's Indian Summer — September's End

Last Day of Summer In The Surf Today

Indian Summer Day -- Splish!

Indian Summer Day -- Splash!

Seven Sunburnt Last Mohicans!

Seven out of sunscreen Last Mohicans A Drowning!

Help us! Save us!

Six Irish Setters with Sunstroke!

Stroke! Stroke! —- The Dead Man's Float!

Five Little League Teams In A Tug of War!

Splish! Splash!

Four Boy Scouts In A Kayak!

Three Unknown Sailors On Shore Leave!

Two Communists Have Cramps!

One of Each Sank In The Icy Blue Sea

(Back) In Nineteen Forty Somethin'

(When) That Famous Tropical Heatwave

(Put) The Lifeguards To The Test

(When) The Beach was Full of Millions

(And) The Lifeguards Got No Rest

THE END

BECOMING BETTIE PAGE

By Dick D. Zigun & Chicava Roslyn Tate

CHICAVA ROSLYN TATE Chicava is an ecdysiast, actor, producer, and writer/director. She holds an MFA from Goddard College focused on sacred sexuality, spirituality, performance art, and on Black Burlesque herstory. As an artist in residence at Joe's Pub at the Public Theater, she produced The Dirty Honey Shake, a live blues & jazz burlesque revue. BGB's annual show at the Brooklyn Museum was a crowd favorite

PRODUCTION HISTORY

BECOMING BETTIE PAGE was developed at the Shooting Gallery Arts Annex in Coney Island, Brooklyn in 2018. The Workshop opened April 22nd and ran seven performances, presented by Coney Island USA partially funded by NYC Cultural Affairs and performed by the Funhouse Philosophers Theater Company.

Co-Written and Produced by Dick D. Zigun.

Co-Written and Directed by Chicava Roslyn Tate.

Scenic and Costume Design by Kate Dale.

CAST

Seedy Edie as Bettie Page

Tomike Ogugua as Jerry Tibbs

John Crandall as Al Falcon

Arron Lloyd as Champion Jack Dupree

Nancy Ellen Reinstein as Mary Fish

Gigi Surreal and Nucomme as Burlesque Dancers

TIME AND PLACE

1950's - Coney Island: Beach, Bluebird Casino, Tirza's Wine Bath

CAST OF HISTORICAL CHARACTERS

JERRY TIBBS - Black, Male, 30-40, NYPD Sergeant/Photographer

BETTIE PAGE - White, Female, 27-year-old Nashville beauty divorced in San Francisco and now moved to NYC

CHAMPION JACK DUPREE - Black, Male, 40 Bluebird's Boogie Woogie house piano player Hawaiian shirt, gold earrings and Star of David; perspiring profusely full time every day. He was a POW in Japan

MARY (FISH) HOOD/TIRZA - White, Female, 30ish, Polish Ohio Waitress who "drinks like a fish" and dances at Tirza's P/T ALSO- Tirza Burlesque performer and club owner

AL (Your Pal) FALCON - White, Male, Jewish , 40-50, Proprietor and MC at Coney Island's Longest Bar/Rhythm & Blues Nightclub : The Bluebird Casino

SCENE 1 - AIRPORT

(Spotlight on the midsection of a woman's hands with pamphlets in them. She's wearing a modest floral dress. She's at the airport to proselytize and save folks. She's working very hard at it.)

BETTIE

Hi sir, I'm just out her sharing the word of God with folks at the airport today. May I give you a pamphlet and tell you about how Jesus saved my life?

Ma'am how are you today? I hope you are having lovely travels. Are you saved? Can I talk to you a moment?

I'm out here today at the airport for Jerry Falwell's mission. Are you saved? Do you know the word of God? He sent his only begotten son to save us and I just want to spread the good news.

(Black Out.)

SCENE 2 - CONEY ISLAND BEACH AND BOARDWALK

(NYPD Sergeant JERRY TIBBS is working out on the beach.)

TIBBS

(In Bathing Trunks & Police Cap Working Out with Dumbbells.)

Hup-2-3-4

I Look Good In Swim Trunks

Hup-2-3-4

I Look Good In Muscles

Hup-2-3-4

A Harlem Cop

A Sergeant

Hup-2-3-4

A Coney Island Polar Bear

Hup-2-3-4

A Photo Bug

With Pin-Up Eyes

Hup-2-3-4

There's a Model Pin-Up I Spy

(He notices BETTIE struck by her beauty he strategizes his approach...puts a shirt on over his workout gear and grabs his camera. Striking up a conversation.)

TIBBS

Hi pretty lady how are you today? I was wondering if I may take your picture? Or rather I'm sorry, what's your name? I'm Sargent Jerry Tibbs NYPD. I'm not just a cop, I'm also almost the World's Best Pin-Up Photographer.

BETTIE

(Tickled and instantly at ease.)

I'm BETTIE, pleasure to make your acquaintance Officer Tibbs. You say you'd like to take my picture? Pin-up like as in Betty Grable? Why I'd like to be that famous. I'm an actress too wouldn't you know.

TIBBS

(Laughs.)

That famous? Have you heard of Camera Clubs?

BETTIE

What's a Camera Club?

TIBBS

It's a group of hobby photographers. Real cool progressive folks, all races, all walks of life. We get together, go out to the country or book a studio and pay models to pose for us.

BETTIE

You pay you say?

TIBBS

Of course, it's fun but its work. Hey, listen How bout we go around to the Bluebird and talk about it?

(Gestures that it's nearby.)

BETTIE

Sure! Sounds good.

(BETTIE and TIBBS walk to the Bluebird. TIBBS takes a few pictures of BETTIE along the way.)

SCENE 3 – BLUEBIRD CASINO

(CHAMPION JACK DUPREE plays some boogie-woogie tune in the style of Shakin' Mother For you.)

AL FALCON

(Larger than life.)

Welcome to The BlueBird Casino, Coney Island's Rhythm and Blues Nightclub featuring Coney Island's Longest Bar & Boogie Woogie Boxing Legend: Champion Jack Dupree on the keys. I'm Al (Your Pal) Falcon, Proprietor & MC of the BlueBird.

(Acknowledges BETTIE & TIBBS entering).

AL FALCON

(To Audience.)

That damn Tibbs. I shoulda been a cop. I mean the pull on the ladies these guys have is ridiculous. Did you see that woman he just walked in with? For Christ-sake. Why do cop pick-up lines work better than I'll make you a star pick-up lines. Jeez!

(BETTIE starts tapping her feet to the music. A born dancer music is hard for her to resist.)

BETTIE

This music is great. Hey let's dance.

(BETTIE doesn't wait for TIBBS she gets up and starts to boogie.)

TIBBS

What'll you have to drink?

BETTIE

A soda would be great. I'm not a drinker.

(MARY FISH the Waitress brings them drinks, She gives BETTIE the once over as she dances.)

(CHAMPION JACK DUPREE finishes the songs and acknowledges BETTIE.)

CHAMPION JACK

Where'd you learn to dance?

BETTIE

Where'd you learn to play like that?

CHAMPION JACK

In an orphanage in New Orleans. But I asked you first.

(BETTIE sits down with CHAMPION JACK at the piano.)

BETTIE

An orphanage, was it awful?

CHAMPION JACK

Being a Japanese prisoner of war was definitely worse than the Colored Waifs Home in New Orleans. Let me tell ya. So where'd you get your moves?

BETTIE

Dancing just makes me happy. I'm not a professional. Acting and modeling are my pursuits. I love salsa, dancing in all the clubs in Times Square. I can't decide if I should ask about the orphanage or the war. I...I was in an orphanage once too...I certainly didn't get my dancing there.

CHAMPION JACK

I got music and a family from the orphange, a brother in Louis Armstrong, a father Willie Hall, him and Tuts Washington took me under their wing and I hit the road.

BETTTIE

Where'd ya play?

CHAMPION JACK

All around, listen and you can hear the sound of the railroad – the route from New Orleans to Chicago, a little St. Louie Mix all that up with that uptown Harlem style! And boom we're all swimming in Coney Island!

BETTIE

Why do they call you Champion Jack Dupree?

CHAMPION JACK

Because I am. These boogie woogie blues hands came out of Golden Gloves. Joe Louis convinced me I was meant for boxing. He was right – I'm a champion.

BETTIE

I'd better go visit with Mr. Tibbs

(She stands and gives CHAMPION JACK a military salute.)

Thank you for serving in the great war. I look forward to many a dance.

CHAMPION JACK

I'll be glad to keep you dancing lady.

(BETTIE bops her way back to the table with TIBBS.)

TIBBS

Wow, you fit right in. And you've got some moves. What's your story?

BETTIE

Born and raised in Nashville. Married my high school sweetheart. He went off to the war. I started teaching but the boys were a little too grown, whistling and fresh. When my husband came back we moved to San Francisco. We tried, but we just didn't work anymore.

TIBBS

Ah, the wild divorcee are we?

BETTIE

Not hardly wild! But I do love life and I'm pursuing my dreams. I did some modeling before in San Francisco, but I don't have any pictures. I tried LA, it's not for me. Figured, try New York.

TIBBS

You chose the right place. . I have a feeling about you.

BETTIE

Being in New York feels like an unavoidable love affair, a passion that had to be.

Are you really going to shoot my portfolio?

TIBBS

Yes, ma'am. Let's meet up this week and from there I'll introduce you to my buddy Cass Carr's photo club. He's up in Harlem. Great shooter and great musician too.

BETTIE

Music and photos, sounds promising

(MARY brings fresh drinks.)

Where'd you find the pretty lady Tibbs?

TIBBS

Working out on the beach - ya know I'm always on the lookout for models

MARY

Yes you are...

Welcome to the Bluebird, I'm Mary Fish I'm Coney Island famous if I do say, burlesque dancer, singer, philosopher of humor. Where ya from?

BETTIE

I'm from Nashville.

MARY

A southern gal that just feels comfortable hanging out with black fellas she just met on the beach...aren't you a rare bird.

TIBBS

Mary, I swear, you got no filter.

MARY

Tell us something we didn't know Tibbs.

(They all laugh MARY continues.)

You know I'm curious. I like to know what's going on behind people's eyes. You don't mind do you kid?

BETTIE

No, it's fine, I'm a southern gal but I've left those ways behind. After my divorce I took a job as a secretary in Haiti. I fell in love with a man and the people. The revolution started and it all fell apart. But Haiti changed me.

TIBBS

Haiti! Wow, full of surprises

MARY

Well aren't you a woman of the world. But I'll tell you what I tell all my girls - Protect your flower.

BETTIE

My Flower?

MARY

Yes sweetie, the flower between your legs.

(she eyes TIBBS and TIBBS laughs it off.)

TIBBS

I have no intentions on the lady's flower Mary
Bettie, Mary tells no lies.

BETTIE

Trust you me, I've been through some shit and I surely will protect my FLOWER! Thanks for looking out Mary

MARY

Anytime, I like you kid. I get paid to just take my clothes off and dance!

(They close the tab with MARY and get set to leave.)

TIBBS

Bettie, models are protected and safe at Camera Clubs. No creeps, I'll protect you and get you paid. Between that and the portfolio I make you, you'll be on your way.

BETTIE

Thanks Jerry, I had a blast at the Bluebird.

TIBBS

My pleasure. See you later this week.

(TIBBS and BETTIE part ways for the night. She thinks for a moment...)

BETTIE

Protection. Ha! I needed protection from my drunk daddy when I was ten years old. I needed protection that night under the Delancey bridge. Wasn't no cops around.

I just thought it'd be fun. Nothing bad had ever happened to me like that in New York. I'm walking along Times Square and a fella asks if I want to go dancing.

I say, Yes, hop in the car thinking it's safe because its him, me and another couple. The girl says, "hi," and we take off. So stupid. A little Nashville girl thinking she can just jump in cars with strangers and go dancing. The Next thing I know four more men get in and by the time we take all them turns on the road, I know I'm not going dancing.

Then we park the car somewhere under the Delancey bridge. The gal and guy in the front seat get out. That woman helped them run a train on me. What a mess of hell she is.

I tell um, I've got my period so I can't do that right now. Those monsters sure did make me give them all head. Groping at my body. Then just threw me onto the street, like an empty bottle of liquor. Those monsters left me for dead. I am never going to forget that night.

I came back to anyway...

Momma didn't want me to. But I had to. There's something in New York for me and I mean to get it. I don't know what it is but there's no way I'm missing it.

SCENE 4 – PHOTOSHOOT WITH TIBBS

(Flash bulbs are going off. BETTIE and TIBBS are in the studio shooting pictures. The first pre-bangs pictures Tibbs did of BETTIE appear on projections. TIBBS takes a few photos of BETTIE then stops and studies her for a long moment)

TIBBS

You're doing great BETTIE. Such a natural you love the camera and it loves you.

(He keeps shooting but then, stops.)

Something's not right...Something is just off perfect.

BETTIE

NOT Perfect?

My Hourglass curves? Perfect

My Blue eyes? Perfect

My Raven Hair?

Perfect

My Girl Next Door Smile?

Perfect

I work out 3 times a week and you're gonna tell me something isn't perfect?

What's not perfect?

Degree from Vanderbilt, a straight A student to top it all off...

What's NOT perfect?

TIBBS

(He sighs a little laughter, realizing.)

Your forehead, the camera doesn't like the glare on your big forehead. To get to PERFECT would you consider cutting bangs? Your hair, your face would look better in bangs.

TOMIKE OGUGUA as Jerry Tibbs tells SEEDY EDIE as Bettie Page that her forehead is too shiny. Photo by Norman Blake.

BETTIE

Well sure why not. I've been wearing my hair this way all my life, never thought to change it. Let's give it a go.

(TIBBS hands BETTIE scissors she steps behind the curtain as if entering the bathroom and we hear her cut her hair. BETTIE Comes from behind curtain...)

Bangs like this? What do you think? Does the camera think I'm perfect now? Perfect with my hair cut in bangs?

(TIBBS takes more pictures.)

Yes, I think yes. The camera is so in love with you. Now, You just be your natural self.

(Flashbulb effects fills the space and pictures appear on the screen.)

TOMIKE OGUGUA as Jerry Tibbs watches SEEDY EDIE cut her hair into bangs. Photo by Norman Blake.

SCENE 5 – BLUEBIRD CASINO

(CHAMPION JACK plays a boogie tune as BETTIE and TIBBS settle into their seats they share the first pictures of new BETTIE Page with the signature bangs with AL, CHAMPION JACK and MARY.Early pictures of BETTIE with bangs come up on the screen.)

TIBBS

What do you think Bettie?

BETTIE

Well, I'm still getting used to my hair but I like um. Tibbs you're a damn good photographer.

(AL comes by to be nosy and see the pictures.)

AL FALCON

Good? They're fantastic! Do you even see yourself lady? You are going to ah, inspire many a man I tell ya. You're a gifted girl. You've got a future ahead of you. What are you doing tomorrow?

BETTIE

I'll be back typing at Rockefeller Center. I might get discovered in Times Square.

AL FALCON

How do you know the day you met Tibbs wasn't the day that changed the rest of your life?

BETTIE

I'll think about it.

CHAMPION JACK

Yup, those flicks and that cute new doo will get you some boyfriends and new husband too.

BETTIE

I don't know about anymore husbands. One was enough for me.

MARY

Husbands come, husbands go that's the story of life. Hey you, Sergeant Shutterbug, I'm taking you and your prisoner with the new bangs and the gams to Coney Island's most underdressed attraction, Tirza's Wine Bath. Heck, I'm treating all of you! It's three blocks down the road...follow m e.

(Lighting Transitions to create Tirza's.)

SCENE 6 – TIRZA'S WINE BATH

(BETTIE, TIBBS, AL, MARY, and CHAMPION JACK DUPREE go to Tirza's Wine Bath

MARY becomes TIRZA, AL voices the JUDGE and then AL becomes the OUTSIDE TALKER at Tirza's and pitches the various attractions of the place.)

AL

Tirza's Wine Bath - The more you clap the more they take off. C'mon over here buddy: As you can see this is an Adult Show where almost anything goes. Whips & Paddles & Spankings & Mouth Gags & Stockings & Garters & Stiletto High Heels. They're going to twitch it and twatch it while you watch it! Shake it up one side and roll it down the other, this show is guaranteed to make the old feel young and the young just want a feel! It's hotter than a cowboy's pistol shooting up the hill on the Fourth of July!

A Judge called it the most indecent Skin Show in New York. To which Tirza replied,

(MARY FISH morphs into TIRZA.)

TIRZA

"My presentation takes us back to the year 200 BC in Athens, very beautiful, very educational." We drink wine because we worship Bacchus. We dance. Come in and see them dance. There's a lovely gal in there right now doing the flower dance... (gestures with hands) she wears one on the east side, one on the west side, and one all the way down by canal street. Then the petals begin to fall and before you know it, you'll see the whole.... entire show! You'll be standing up straighter than the center pole of the tent!

AL

The Judge said Tirza you're going to jail!

TIRZA

OK Judgie no more bump and grind when the kids are around – when the kiddies come around my bump and grind gals only sway so is that ok?

AL

Tirza's is still open. She paid off the cops, I mean they were her biggest fans! It's Coney Island. Nobody cares.

(AL clears the way for the show to begin.)

TIRZA

Welcome to Tirza's Wine Bath. I'm sure you will enjoy the show

(Opening - Temptation)

(Girl in wine bath emerges and sexily bathes herself with a sponge. She poses lazily in the tub before slowly rising to dry off with towel and/or put on a dressing gown. As she saunters off a gypsy dancer enters wearing veils/ panel skirt and twirls and shimmies about acknowledging the "audience". Lastly enters the Asian glamour girl or traditionally dressed Asian dancer who poses and parades about.)

(Dancers continue as we join the Bluebird crew at their table.)

TIRZA

So whatcha think BETTIE? Do they do like that in Tennessee?

BETTIE

They sure don't dance like that in Nashville not even in Memphis on Beale Street.

TIBBS

Irving & his sister Paula Klaw in Sheepshead Bay pay models for mail order cheesecake pinups. Would you do a little stockings stilettos & bondage?

BETTIE

Really? Hmm, I'll try it. Does it pay better than being a secretary?

AL FALCON

You betcha it does, like $150 an hour.

BETTIE

Are you serious?! Good lord!

(Mary re-emerges welcoming/ heavily inviting BETTIE to join the group on the stage. They touch her all over and sway her hips as to Show her how to figure 8 and position her arms.)

CHAMPION JACK

Oh trust you me, people will pay for the freaky fetish stuff. People like weird shit...it fights the blues.

(Then she's off and taking the lead parading and posing. Holding a classic BETTIE pose the group strips 1-2 pieces. And they head over to BETTIE to remove her T-shirt dress revealing the sexy Dominatrix outfit. She checks herself out and then MARY hands her the whip. She parades again to center stage with the whip and they watch mesmerized in tableau. Holds a breath teasing with the whip then BETTIE twirls and poses and happily cracks the whip and the group strips. Repeat again.)

TIBBS

Irving's got lawyers and business all around the country paying him to make this kinda stuff. Ya know give it a whirl.

(BETTIE saunters to stage right as the group forms a line pasties revealed walks closer snaps her fingers and they ripple into a laid position head on the back of the person before them hips moving slightly. She twirls again and cracks the whip this time reacting as if they felt the leather with much ecstasy and sensuality. BETTIE walks by running her finger (or whip tendrils) across their bodies as she passes and they fidget and giggle. Flash bulbs go off in constant flairs One by one each rise and flutter over to surround BETTIE slowly stripping away the final costume bits and finally melting around her as she raises her hands and whip high in exultation in the final tableau.)

(The final image in the number is that of BETTIE in Leopard Print with Whip – Snap of whip sound marks the height of BETTIE PAGE's career.)

SCENE 7 – BACK AT THE BLUEBIRD

(BETTIE counting cash as she bops to the music in the Bluebird.)

TIBBS

What's a girl to do with all that cash.

BETTIE

Buy you a drink Daddy-O. You made it all possible!

(BETTIE gives TIBBS a friendly kiss on the cheek.)

AL

Good lord Bettie! You're all the rage. You're in every below board magazine Pin-ups, sweaty Fetish mags. You are the lady in the unmarked mail package.

TIBBS

So Irving is bringing in the loot! Is Bondage your thing now? A bang cut and a spanking have made you famous.

BETTIE

Me and the girls did not even know who wants these crazy pictures. But it's how we get Irving to pay us. Do people actually dig this stuff? It's so much work. Who has time for all that when you could just be getting it on. Men like to see women tied up, helpless, spanking each other. Anyway, it's some kind of acting gig.

SEEDY EDIE as Bettie Page taking off her stockings. Photo by Norman Blake.

(MARY brings drinks to the table.)

MARY

Well isn't that a fancy watch you got.

BETTIE

Isn't it sweet my honey designed it just for me.

MARY

Is this the car maker I've been hearing about you painting the town with?

BETTIE

It's true I'm one lucky lady. I haven't taken the watch off. I just love it so.

MARY

(To Audience.)

This girl...How could you even hate the girl. I mean jeez the looks of her made ya wanna try. But it was clear real quick she wasn't seeing herself in the awe the rest of the world did. It's like she didn't know you couldn't take your eyes off her. She didn't lack esteem, mind ya, oh no. She loved herself. You could tell she liked who she was and felt a right to be who she was.

(Everyone but BETTIE leaves the stage. The jovial atmosphere is interrupted by a voice announcement as the scene goes dark.)

SCENE 8 – KEFAUVER HEARINGS

Projection: Archival Senate hearings with audio.

(BETTIE sitting isolated. Other actors cover BETTIE and redress her more conservative.)

AL

A young man was found dead today from an apparent self-strangulation after being exposed to obscene and pornographic material published by one Irving Klaw of Brooklyn, New York. The promiscuous works feature in particular a model named Bettie Mae Page. The Kefauver Senate Committee investigation into pornography hereby demands your appearance and testimony in the matter of your participation in the endangerment of youth. By working for Mr. Klaw's business you participated in the illegal interstate commerce of pornographic and sadistic imagery.

In summary:

"It's rather difficult, unless one has an understanding of the particular perversion involved, for the average person to completely understand and notice the pornographic nature of Klaw's material." Obscenity shall be defined as content that "using community standards...appeals to prurient interest and which is utterly without redeeming social importance." "I know it when I see it."

(BETTIE sits in a darken space as the McCarthy hearings sounds play in the background. She becomes visibly diminished. A dancer brings BETTIE a phone.)

BETTIE

Hi baby, how are you. I can't wait to see you.

(Voice on the other end of the line tells her it's over that he's going back to his wife.)

Oh...why? Why now are you giving it another try? I thought we were happy. I thought you were happy? Why are you leaving me? What did I do wrong? We were going to have a future.

(Dancer returns and takes phone.)

SCENE 9 – BLUEBIRD CASINO 1956-57

(THE BLUEBIRD CASINO but somber CHAMPION JACK plays a tune in the style of Careless Love.)

(Tibbs pulls up a chair by BETTIE and sits quietly feeling her pain with her. She starts talking.)

BETTIE

He left me Tibbs. He went back to his wife.

TIBBS

Ah, Bettie. I am so so sorry. He's making a mistake y'all were meant for each other and deep inside he knows that.

BETTIE

More than any of em. I loved him. He made me feel more alive. So ok, like he could hold all of me. Men, they think they want a force of nature, but they just want a regular gal cooking, cleaning, and waiting for them to get home.

Why so they can lay on their back and take some thrusts of a dwindling passion and put up a perfect family show.

That is never gonna be me. I'm Bettie Mae Page of Nashville, Tennessee, I'm my own and I am free.

(A dancer brings a suitcase on stage and sets it next to BETTIE. After the dancer leaves BETTIE picks it up and walks upstage center.)

TIBBS

(To Audience.)

She was just so fine.

I mean Bettie was one of those special kinda women. What you'd call a nine cow woman. Not a 2 cow or a 3 cow but a 9 cow give up the whole farm to get this gal kinda fine. A man should have to lay out the whole spread of what they'll do for her, her whole life long, fine. White, black or otherwise she was one of the most striking women I've ever encountered. I could always see there was a lot on her heart, but more than that I saw the spark of her spirit. And I knew right away it was a spark that could light the world on fire. To see a man put out that spark right when her whole career's been ripped away from her, it hard. Bettie deserved better.

SCENE 10 - BETTIE BREAKS

Projection: Starts Crucifix - Blues song à Heavy Metal atmosphere à Ava Maria à Jerry Falwell preaching.

Collapses

SCENE 11 - BETTIE IS AN ICON

Projection: Bettie Page historic footage

(Meanwhile off-stage BETTIE changes into a Nurse Bettie uniform underneath her house dress.)

Scene 12 - BORN AGAIN BETTIE

(She returns to Proselytizing at the airport.)

(Projection: Airport with people chatter sounds Black Stage with Spotlight on hands.)

BETTIE

Hi sir, I'm just out her sharing the word of God with folks at the airport today. May I give you a pamphlet and tell you about how Jesus saved my life? Ma'am how are you today? I hope you are having lovely travels. Are you saved? Can I talk to you a moment?

I'm out here today at the airport for Jerry Falwell's mission. Are you saved? Do you know the word of God? He sent his only begotten son to save us and I just want to spread the good news.

(CHAMPION JACK walks on stage and hands Bettie a letter instead of taking a Jesus pamphlet. She opens it as he recites the letter.)

CHAMPION JACK

Dear Bettie,

My name is Dave Lee Stevens.

I am so glad to finally find you and learn that you are well. Back in the 80s I created a comic called The Rocketeer. I based the hero's girlfriend off you. You have inspired me since the first time I saw a picture of you.

Do you know that you're a star Bettie?

Fashion magazines recreate your look on armies of models.

Women cut their bangs just like yours. They learn to walk in high heals because of you. You inspire tight clothes, daring attitudes, and the living out of fantasies.

You're on everything from t-shirts to lunchboxes.

I thank your brother for putting us in touch.

It would mean everything to me to meet you and show you the legend you've become.

Sincerely,

Dave

(LIGHT CUE: Blackout.)

SEEDY EDIE as Bettie Page on the beach. Photo by Norman Blake.

SCENE 13 – BETTIE ON THE BEACH IN CALIFORNIA 1990s-2000s

Projection: California Beach.

What if I hadn't of gone back to New York. What if I had just stayed home with momma. A broken, scared and shutdown woman. So many things want to break a woman. Even the woman herself. Or even what if I had stayed southern racist I woulda tried to have Jerry arrested for talking to me, and he was a cop. But my mind was open so my life opened up to me. I woulda missed my destiny. I didn't know it was my destiny when it was happening, you never know that – That's not how life works...most of getting through life is taking a guess. How could I know one day some young fella would take me to a store and there's a whole display of me. Been struggling for years - come to find out I'm a million-dollar business. I ain't always made good choices but a lot of them sure were fun.

(BETTIE stands and starts dancing to a tune in the style of Dupree's "Nasty Boogie.")

THE END

LILLIE'S WORLD IN WAX

By Dick D. Zigun

PRODUCTION HISTORY

LILLIE'S WORLD IN WAX was developed at the World In Wax Musee' in Coney Island, Brooklyn, NY in 1981. Dick Zigun served as a voluntary Artist-In-Residence the entire 1981 Season during which several attempts were made to "re-install" Lillie Santangelo's "voice" back into the carnival cacophony that is the Coney Midway.

Part One:

WORLD IN WAX MUSEE' OUTDOOR GRIND TAPE ANNOUNCEMENT

Based On The Art & Words of Lillie Santangelo

Was recorded by Voice Actor, Bill Bixby and broadcast outside the Main Entrance the entire 1981 Season.

In 1982 Dick Zigun performed the text (with slide projections) at New Dramatists in Manhattan as part of a "Poetry By Playwrights" event.

Part Two:

THE FULL-MOON STRANGLER...THE FIVE-YEAR-OLD MOTHER AND...CONEY ISLAND LIL

Was published as the full-page cover story of the DAILY NEWS weekend section on August 28, 1981

Part Three:

SECRETS OF THE WAX MUSEE'

Was performed October 31, 1981 at the World In Wax itself concluding an all day site specific festival called TRICKS & TREATS AT THE WAX MUSEE'. The performance showcased some 50 wax heads retrieved from the Musee's storage rooms. The performance was Directed, Designed and written by Zigun. Dimitri Mantis and Ross Steinhardt also performed.

PART ONE

WORLD IN WAX MUSEE'
Outdoor Grind Tape Announcement
Based On The Art & Words Of Lillie Santangelo

Step up, Step up into the World in Wax; New York's only wax museum, the only attraction of its kind in Coney Island. In fact, the oldest wax museum in the US of A. Since 1926 we have brought you famous people of the past and present. We have ill-famed people who teach you that crime does not pay and famous people of stage and politics and sports who teach you the beauty of life. It's an educational show, it's a horror show. It's real. It's real life. The World in Wax. It's so real you'd think they were about to start talking.

See John Lennon, the number one Beatle. Muhammed Ali, the Greatest. Elvis Presley, the King of Rock and Roll. These are not statues, they are not cold marble statues nor are they bronze which you see in the parks. This is a wax show, a living memory in honor of great people, in warning of bad. Here they are memorable, you will never forget them. You might think that the famous are breathing. Step into the World in Wax and visit our stage.

Step up, step up into the World in Wax and see Roberto Clemente, the idol of Puerto Rico. Roberto Clemente, the all-star outfielder, the superstar baseball player for the world champion Pittsburgh Pirates. Roberto Clemente, the man who died on a mission of mercy. Roberto Clemente, the Pirate with a heart of gold who was bringing food and clothing to the people he loved. You will see him in his baseball uniform as you might have seen him on television or at a ballgame. Roberto Clemente, in our own baseball hall of fame. Roberto Clemente, who died when his plane crashed into the sea. His body was never found but right here, right now, you can see him here on our stage.

Step up, step up into the World in Wax and see the two headed baby. Yes, a two headed baby, born New Year's Day at Selly Oak Hospital, Birmingham, England. A strange baby girl born to an American serviceman and his English wife. The baby has two normally shaped heads, two necks, two stomachs and two sets of lungs... all joined to the very same little body. Each head breathes, eats and cries independently of the other. See the surprised expression on the shocked nurse's face.

See the grave, concerned doctor. The two headed baby living her strange double life of 48 hours. The two headed baby, right here, right now, on our stage.

Step up, step up into the World in Wax and see World War Two over again. See the great General MacArthur the way he looked when he said: "I shall return!" See Madam Chiang Kai-shek, the beautiful woman they called Dragon Lady. You can relive World War Two, right here, right now, on our stage.

See John Lennon, the number one Beatle, Muhammed Ali, the greatest, Elvis Presley, the king of rock and roll. It's real. It's real life. The World in Wax. It's so real you'd think they were about to start talking.

Step up, step up into the World in Wax and see the Duke and Duchess of Windsor. The Duke who should have been King. The man who gave up his throne for love. He could have been King but he wanted to marry a commoner. The Duke and Duchess of Windsor, right here, right now, on our stage.

Step up, step up into the World in Wax and see the great Nat King Cole. The fabulous singer, the smooth entertainer, Nat King Cole, the most adorable person on stage. The man who made famous such songs as "Mona Lisa"' and "Chestnuts Roasting On An Open Fire" and other big hits. Nat King Cole, the singer, right here, right now, on our stage.

Step up, step up into the World in Wax and see the smartest man of our time, Albert Einstein. The man they call the Father of our own Atomic Age. Albert Einstein, the genius who explained space, explained the atom, who said: "E=mC2," Albert Einstein, the genius whose violin teacher said he could not count or keep time. Albert Einstein, a brilliant man, who knew the secrets of the universe. Did he tell us too much? You decide, right here, right now, on our stage.

Wax figures of the Duke & Duchess of Windsor photos by Costa Mantis.
Courtesy The Coney Island Museum, Brooklyn, N.Y.

Wax figure of Albert Einstein. Photo by Costa Mantis. Courtesy The Coney Island Museum, Brooklyn, N.Y.

See John Lennon, the #1 Beatle. Muhammed Ali, The Greatest! Elvis Presley, the King of Rock n Roll. It's real. It's real life. The World in Wax. It's so real, you'd think they were about to start talking.

Step up, step up into the World in Wax and see Richard Speck. The man who murdered eight student nurses on a hot summer night in Chicago. Imagine... murdering eight student nurses in Chicago on a hot summer night... Richard Speck. A madman? A deranged man? Richard Speck, still in prison Should he rot in his cell or should he go free? Richard Speck, right here, right now, on our stage.

Step up, step up into the World in Wax and see six great American presidents. See Ulysseus S. Grant, the Civil War hero and Dwight Eisenhower, that other great patriotic general who did so much in the Second World War. A patriotic display of American presidents in wax. See Warren G. Harding, Harry S. Truman, William McKinley and the late President Kennedy. It's an educational show, right here, right now, on our stage.

See John Lennon, the #1 Beatle. Muhammed Ali, the Greatest. Elvis Presley, the King of Rock n Roll. It's real. It's real life.

Step up, step up into the World in Wax and see the three American martyrs to justice. President John Kennedy, the Reverend Martin Luther King, Jr. and Senator Robert Kennedy. Black and white, alive in the White House, together, making plans in the Civil Rights days. The believed, together, 'We Shall Overcome". "We Shall Overcome"', that's what Martin Luther King, Jr. is saying as the two Kennedy brothers listen. Three great men who tried to stop violence, each of them shot down in great tragedy. "We Shall Overcome"', that was their philosophy. Not with hatred but with education, peace & love. President Kennedy, Senator Kennedy and Rev. Martin Luther King, Jr.

Right here, right now, on our stage.

Step up, step up into the World in Wax, but do not, I repeat, do NOT look at Hickman "The Fox"' unless you have a strong heart. Consider yourself warned! People have fainted when they looked at Hickman "The Fox" committing his crime. "'The Fox"', finally captured after one of the most sensational manhunts in history... but too late for poor twelve year old Marion Parker. Hickman

"The Fox" paid for his crime in the gas chamber of the State of California. "Crime does not pay. Hickman "The Fox"' if you can face him." Right here, right now, on our stage.

It's real. It's real life. The World in Wax. It's so real you'd think they were about to start talking.

Step up, step up into the World in Wax and see Felisa Rincon, the well loved Mayoress of San Juan, the capital city of Puerto Rico. Felisa Rincon, Mayoress for over 20 years. Well known for her civic and political leadership and her great work in humanitarian activities. The woman from Puerto Rico who became an Ambassador of Goodwill on her many trips to cities in the United States. Felisa Rincon, well loved by her people, right here, right now on our stage.

Step up, step up into the World in Wax and see the King of Rock n Roll. Elvis the Pelvis, the one and only great Elvis Presley. Come in and see Elvis. Come in and sing with Elvis. Come in and swing with Elvis. Come in and rock, rock with Elvis. Yes, the King is Back, and you will see him right now on our stage. Elvis Presley, the King, dressed in the same jeweled costume he wore during his concerts. We will return your money if Elvis is not wearing his jeweled costume. Elvis Presley, the King, right here, right now, on our stage.

See John Lennon, the #1 Beatle. Muhammed Ali, The Greatest. Elvis Presley, the King of Rock n Roll. The World in Wax. It's so real you'd think they were about to start talking.

Step up, step up into the World in Wax and see Fred Thompson, a 59 year old man who killed and raped four year old Edith, at play, in Manhattan. Crazy Fred Thompson, ruled insane, who escaped the electric chair and still lives in prison. Fred Thompson, see him sit in his cell. Imagine... sitting in prison for life. Fred Thompson, right here, right now on our stage.

Step up, step up into the World in Wax and see NY's great men of the past. See Governor Dewey and see Mayor Fiorello LaGuardia - the mayor for the little people, the one who read the comics over the radio during the newspaper strike. Just two of the famous and infamous people you can see right here, right now, on our stage.

Step up, step up into the World in Wax and see Lina Medina, the world's youngest mother. Imagine, a little girl giving birth to a baby boy at the age of five. Imagine...a little girl giving birth to a baby at the age of five years. Yes, see the nurse, see the baby and see how the baby's mother is a baby herself. Lina Medina is five years old, only 37 inches tall. She still has her first set of teeth... yet that's her baby son the nurse is holding in the Lima, Peru hospital. The infant, doing fine, weighed almost six pounds at the caesarean birth. Do you believe it? Sixty doctors, sixty doctors watched the strange birth. Lina Medina, the world's youngest mother, right here, right now, you decide for yourself on our stage.

See John Lennon, Muhammed Ali, Elvis Presley. It's real.. It's real life. It's so real you'd think they were about to start talking.

Step up, step up into the World in Wax and see Muhammad Ali, the most famous man in the world. The heavyweight champ who said: "I am the greatest!" and he's still the greatest, right here on our stage. Muhammad Ali, the champ not once, not twice, but three times. The world's greatest fighter. Muhammad Ali, the greatest, right here, right now, on our stage.

Step up, step up into the World in Wax and see John Christie, the perverse Full Moon Strangler. John Christie, the London strangler of blondes. The Full Moon Strangler who selected blonde London prostitutes for his love affairs... and then killed them for their blood... which he drank. The Full Moon Strangler, about to start choking one of his blonde victims. John Christie, the Full Moon Strangler, right here, right now, on our stage.

Step up, step up into the World in Wax and see Ruth Snyder, the very first woman electrocuted by the State of New York. Ruth Snyder and the cold blooded Judd Grey, the man she picked up in a bar. See them committing the deed while her husband innocently sleeps. Ruth Snyder and Judd Grey after her husband's insurance. Ruth Snyder and Judd Grey killing her husband in his sleep on March 20, 1927. Ruth Snyder, the first woman strapped into the electric chair by the State of New York. Crime does not pay. She paid for her crime on January 12, 1928. Ruth Snyder, right here, right now, on our stage.

Step up, step up into the World in Wax and see The Screwdriver Killer, Julio Ramirez Perez. See the thief who hid behind the door when the housewife came home to her upper east side Manhattan apartment on March 30th, 1948. See the Screwdriver Killer, the man who got the electric chair in Sing-Sing Prison, March 1950 to prove, once again, that crime does not pay. The Screwdriver Killer, right here, right now, on our stage.

Step up, step up into the World in Wax and see John Roche, the Rape Killer, about to commit one of his crimes A confessed killer of four or five of his victims, see him stalking his latest victim in the hallway of her apartment building. John Roche, a killer, later arrested and jailed. Another example that crime does not pay. John Roche, inside, right here, right now, on our stage.

Step up, step up into the World in Wax and see the Red Light Bandit, Caryl ("'Carol") Chessman. See him in the gas chamber, about to die on our stage. Caryl Chessman, the Red Light Bandit who assaulted a teenage girl and a semi-paralyzed woman. He was tried, convicted and sentenced to death for kidnapping, a capital crime in the State of California. Come in and see how Caryl Chessman, the Red Light Bandit, paid with his life for the many crimes that he committed. See him strapped into the gas chamber, May 2nd, 1960, the day that he died. The Red Light Bandit, right here, right now, on our stage.

Step up, step up into the World in Wax and see our newest feature attraction. John Lennon, the number one Beatle. The man who started the group. The man who said: "Give Peace A Chance"'. The man gunned down right here in New York: John Lennon, don't ever forget him. John Lennon, a tribute, here on our stage. He is so real, so life like, that many have actually cried when they first saw him. John Lennon, in his famous white suit and white sneakers. The number one Beatle. The greatest Beatle of our time, as he looked in real life. Right here, right now on our stage, our feature at traction!

PART TWO

The Full-Moon Strangler...

The Five-Year-Old Mother and...

CONEY ISLAND LIL

LILLIE SANTANGELO in Ticket Booth , 1981 Photo by Evelyn Zigun. Courtesy The Coney Island Museum, Brooklyn, N.Y.

STEP UP INTO the World in Wax Musee and see the late John Lennon, the Number One Beatle, our newest attraction! yells the little old barker as she hands you a one-dollar ticket and nods you in through her door. Lillie Beatrice Santangelo, New York's own Madame Tussaud, has just unveiled another waxen image at the Coney Island museum she opened in 1926. Inside Lillie's hall of fame, John Lennon's likeness is haunting and hip, successfully Beatle. He is dressed all in white: white suit, white sneakers, "Abbey Road" style. His face is adult, clean shaven. His long hair is parted either side of his wire-rim specs like in the White Album portrait. On his lapel, a peace symbol button; around his neck, simple white beads. "Too bad he was killed, but that's life," Lillie lectures t he crowd.

"We come and we go. We just blow out of this country, this world, like the wind. Here's a man walking home with his wife-all of a sudden it's over. The end. That's what they call the ill wind, I believe." Above the feature attraction hangs an orange and blue banner painted with the motto: ALWAYS SOMETHING NEW! The banner is ancient. The slain Beatle joins Einstein, Eisenhower, Elvis and 43 other exotics. Muhammad Ali. The Full-Moon Strangler Madame Chiang Kai-shek.

The Screwdriver Killer, Mayor LaGuardia. The five-year-old mother, the two-headed baby, electric chair sitters, American martyrs and saints. All lived, made history and filled newspapers. High over the wax tableaus are canvas murals painted with scenes from Dante's Inferno. "I'm just taking from my heart what I have seen in life. A wax show teaches the good things in life and also teaches crime doesn't pay. What makes a person bad? So near and yet so far! What makes a clock tick-bad or good?" Lillie, who is 80, wants to know.

For more than half a century, she has stood in her box office and watched millions of New Yorkers head for the beach. "Coney Island is the greatest resort in the world for poor people. Here you find the people's culture. I encourage that. I bring it to them. This is not a concession. I consider this art!" boasts the gray-haired impresario-half P.T. Barnum, half Grandma Moses.

What would John Lennon, the rock 'n' roll symbolist who once sang "I am the walrus" think of all this? Find a copy of "Double Fantasy", put on side two, and listen to the full album version of

"Watching the Wheels", one of Lennon's last songs. "No longer riding on the merry-go-round..." he sings. Without a formal conclusion, the song drifts into a short interlude. Dubbed over the banjo plucking, that's Lillie at Coney, audibly selling tickets in both English and Spanish. John says something garbled, cryptic, he speaks in reverse. You spin your turntable backward and ruin your record. Lillie says she never met Lennon alive. It puzzles her too.

She did write and ask Yoko Ono for clothes, received none, but was told Yoko laughed. That makes Lillie smile. So how did she get her John Lennon dressed? Hard times have hit Coney, and, like others there, Lillie is proud but poor. The Beatle's outfit came from the East Village and Soho, thanks to a group of New York artists playing shoemaker's elves. They want to see the museum restored and endowed but have no funding yet.

Lennon's booth needs a new backdrop; he now stands in front of Elvis Presley's pink satin. Elvis was moved. Other figures are peeling. Lillie threatens to sell. "I have no hopes for my future," she says. "I'll keep working while I can. When I can't, I retire. God is the boss. I leave it to God."

As she always has. Lillie Beatrice Santangelo was an orphan, adopted by a childless couple who ran a photo studio in World War I days. She would take a 5 a.m. dip in the cold Atlantic and then go to work; she has only an eighth-grade education. At 17, with a $700 loan from her father, she opened her own photo studio. During the roaring '20s she opened two more-one in Steeplechase Park, where she photographed Charlie Chaplin-and another in Manhattan, across from Jack Dempsey's restaurant, where she remembers Red Skeleton escaping from fans who had doused him with beer.

In 1925, Lillie married Ralph Santangelo and traded her cameras for wax. Ralph hired a Swedish sculptor, Sandohl, to make the first 30 figures. Lillie and Ralph ran the wax show together. They lived in Seagate and then, for years, in the Half Moon Hotel on the Boardwalk. In the Half Moon's ballroom, Lillie would meet celebrities like Amelia Earhart and one-eyed Wiley Post. She was there the night the police threw Kid Twist of Murder, Inc., out the window.

She lives now in a Brighton Beach apartment. Her parents, her husband, are gone. Once again, she's alone. No one else is quite like her. No one else knows what she knows. New York has no other wax show. America, none older. She watches over her collection, her folk art. She guards 60 more heads boxed in storage. Her Babe Ruth. Her Hitler. She doesn't know if her fate is a casino, a fire, or her own likeness in wax.

Meanwhile, she's still open for business.

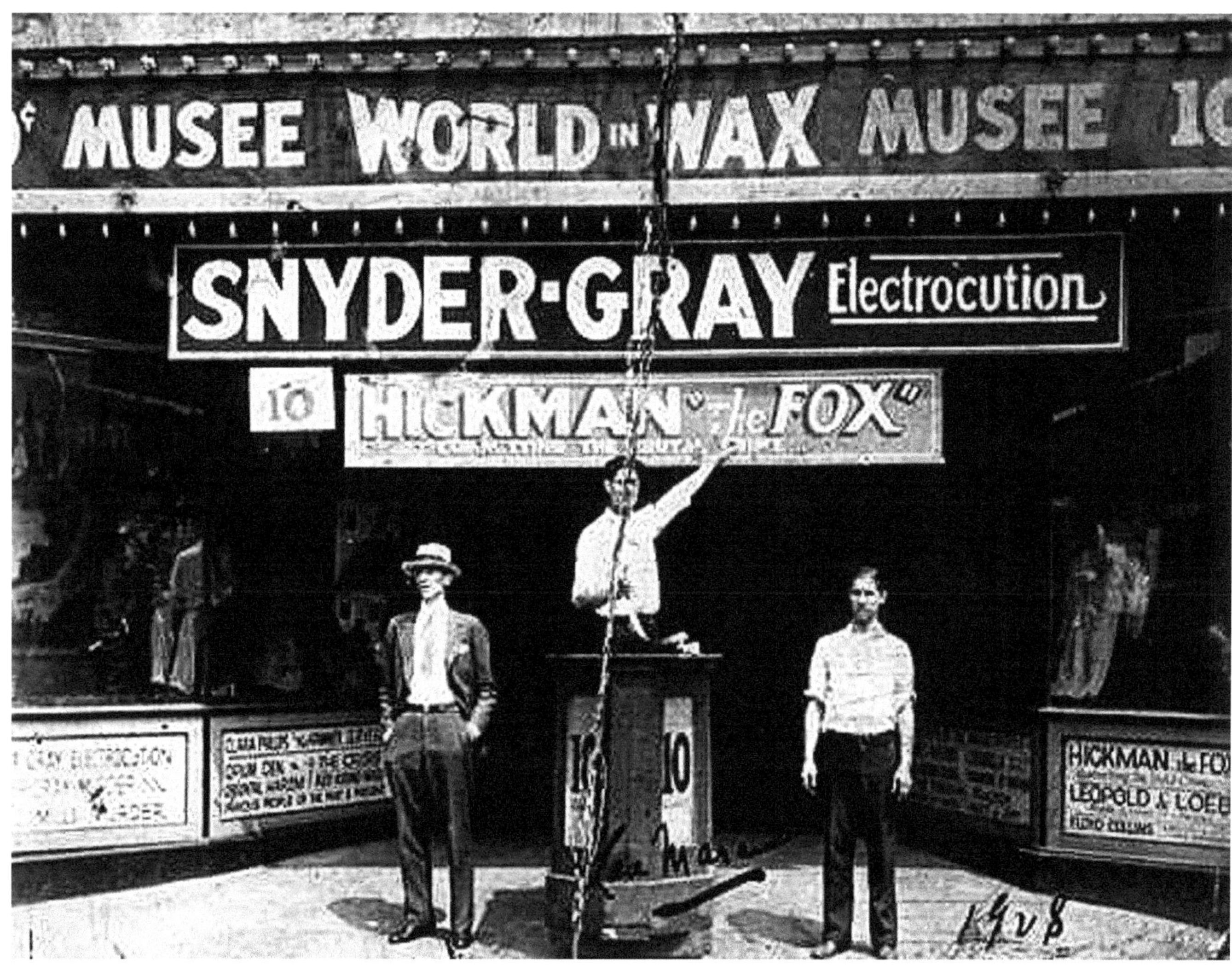

Entrance to World In Wax Musee' circa 1927. Courtesy The Coney Island Museum, Brooklyn, N.Y.

PART THREE

SECRETS OF THE WAX MUSEE'

(CAST: MAN WEARING A DERBY HAT, KEYSTONE COP, CONEY ISLAND TICKET SELLER)

(Band Organ Music)

MAN WEARING A DERBY HAT

Ladies and Gentlemen…things that go bump in the night…this is a Halloween story, a tale for the night when the spirits are out.

We will talk of the dead,

(sound)

we are not holding a séance…

Ladies and gentlemen: relax…if you're not in the mood,

(Clock ticks)

pretend that you're dreaming…that you're hypnotized…or that you've just been strapped into an old amusement park ride…

(Door shuts)

(KEYSTONE COP wheels out a rotating bookcase on wheels Facing the audience the shelves can hold several heads in various poses. Faced away from the audience the rotating bookcase can be changed and reloaded again and again.)

Ladies and gentlemen: trust the ride…don't shut your eyes…

(Whispering)

Let us share a few secrets:

(Carnival music)

Ladies and gentlemen, I am going to share a few secrets...

TICKET SELLER IN TICKET BOOTH

Ladies and gentlemen, here we have: 4 cartoon type characters. Up on top there's Mutt and Jeff from the old cartoon strip. Mutt and Jeff used to be in a display outside when the museum first opened in 1926. You can see them in the old picture on the poster. On your right is Jiggs, the cartoon character from Bringing Up Father. He always wears a top hat and smokes a cigar, gets drunk and runs out of the house on his wife. On your left is a Japanese man from a World War Two display. We don't know if he's from a cartoon strip or not but we included him with the others because he is very cartoon like.

(The bookcase rotates. The Wax heads change, ad. Infinitim)

Ladies and gentlemen, here we have the man who built Yankee Stadium, the great number 3, The Babe, the great home run king. Not only is that the original head, but this is also the uniform we found that the Babe wore for years in this very museum.

Ladies and gentlemen, here we have 4 men with beards. On the bottom we have President Abraham Lincoln, and on the top shelf are 3 men and we don't have any idea who they are. If Mrs. Santangelo or anyone here tonight who remembers who these people were in the museum, please feel free to speak up.

Ladies and gentlemen, here we have the great heavyweight champion, the one; the only, Mr. Joe Louis. Mr. Louis is wearing an army cap because during the war, even though he was heavyweight champion of the world, he fought on our side and that's the way he was on display in this museum. Please notice the fine work on the hands as well as the head.

Ladies and gentlemen, here we have 4 babies. You'll notice that the one in the middle matches the 3 babies on permanent display in the case. If you can imagine a fifth missing baby, you'd have the original display of the famous Dionne Quintuplets, born in Canada during the Depression. In the milk crates are 2 heads from another display of Dionne Quintuplets. We don't know who the baby is on top with the closed eyes.

ROSS STEINHARDT as Narrator presents Babe Ruth's wax head and hands and Yankees uniform. Photo by Cynthia Friedman. Courtesy The Coney Island Museum, Brooklyn, N.Y.

Ladies and gentlemen, here we have 2 possible candidates for the head of Martha Beck. One of these 2 was the head of the woman from Park Slope, Brooklyn who killed her lesbian lover and made New York newspaper headlines.

Ladies and gentlemen, here we have selections from the World In Wax Hollywood Collection. On the top is a local boy, old blue eyes himself, the young Frank Sinatra. On your right is James Dean. On your left is Clark Gable, and in the middle is the old shnozola himself, Jimmy Durante.

Ladies and gentlemen, here we have a display with 4 Black men. On the bottom are 3 of the famous Scotsboro Boys. The Scotsboro Boys were the defendants in an important trial in American history. To this day, many people believe they were not guilty as charged.

DIMITRI MANTIS as Keystone Cop, DICK ZIGUN as MAYOR OF CONEY ISLAND and ROSS STEINHARDT as Narrator with Wax Heads of Frank Sinatra, Jimmy Durante, Clark Gable and James Dean. Photo by Cynthia Friedman. Courtesy The Coney Island Museum, Brooklyn, N .Y.

Ladies and gentlemen, here we have the men who fought World War Two. On the top shelf, Joseph Stalin of the Soviet Union and Winston Churchill of England. Next we have President Franklin Delanor Roosevelt. FDR was the only president elected to 4 terms. Ladies and gentlemen, in the milk crates, Benito Mussolini of Italy and the Nazi villain, Adolf Hitler.

Ladies and gentlemen, here we have 6 dying women. We know who the one on the bottom is but she's the secret. This time we can tell you the 2 dead women in the milk crates were both wives of the pirate Bluebeard. He had 8 wives and liked to keep the bodies of the divorced ones hanging around.

Ladies and gentlemen, here we have the killer. As you can see by the many hands with guns that we found, there have been many more killers in this room. We chose this one to show you tonight as the killer. For 55 years, the World in Wax has presented quite a few killers. The World in Wax had presented the entire history of New York since 1926, killers included. This is the World in Wax. We are the oldest wax museum in the U. S. of A. And a good wax show both teaches you the good things in life and that crime doesn't pay.

Ladies and gentlemen, here we have our last 8 heads in tonight's performance. This display brings the total heads you've seen 50. There are over 50 more heads stored in the back. There are 50 figures on permanent display. This last display before you is of 8 regular people. We don't know who they are, but they're not covered in blood. These people might be butchers or bakers or Indian chiefs. We might have stumbled on Leopold and Loeb or Sacco and Vinzetti, Cinderella, Mother Goose or any of the others we know were once on display out here in Coney Island. Do you know these people?

THE END

DICK ZIGUN & LILLIE SANTANGELO with anonymous wax heads. Photo by Evelyn Zigun. Courtesy The Coney Island Museum, Brooklyn, N.Y.

THE RIDE INSPECTOR'S NIGHTMARE

By Dick D. Zigun

PRODUCTION HISTORY

THE RIDE INSPECTOR'S NIGHTMARE was first developed as a Halloween "Creepshow at The Freakshow" in 2010 and 2011 at Sideshows by the Seashore in Coney Island. The audience followed the Ride Inspector from room to room each change of scene.

Sets by KATE DALE. Environmental Installations by MARIE ROBERTS.

Cast included SCOTT BAKER, CHRIS MIANO, JESSE MIANO, LUIS MICHAELS, ALEJANDRO DUBOIS, and AUDWIN GATHERS.

This theatrical stage version of the show received a Brooklyn Showcase Premiere in 2015 produced by Coney Island, USA. It opened October 5, 2015 and ran 18 performances.

Written and Directed by Dick D. Zigun.

CAST

ZERO BOY, ALFIE BUNZ , NATI THE PATCHWORK GIRL, PRINCESS PAT, PATRICK SALAZAR

Scenic and Costume Design: KATE DALE

Video Mapping Projections: DENNIS CATALFUMO

CAST OF CHARACTERS BASED ON A TRUE STORY

CHIEF RIDE INSPECTOR PATTY MCKAY

DEPUTY CHIEF RIDE INSPECTOR MANNY MADELBAUM

HANDICAPPED WOMAN RIDE INSPECTOR w/ARM BRACE/STICKY FINGERS

BLACK WOMAN RIDE INSPECTOR/MARY MELODY

MALE DEAD BODY RIDE INSPECTOR/JUDGE

All characters dressed in White Lab Coats and Hardhats branded with the logo of NYC DEPT OF BUILDINGS. The Dead Body Inspector wears a black hardhat.

SCENE ONE

(The Locker Room for Ride Inspectors at The Brooklyn Headquarters of the NYC Department of Buildings. It is late Friday night after a full week of work yet two Inspectors, PATTY McKAY and MANNY MANDELBAUM, remain drinking and swapping stories instead of going home to their lives. As the audience enters the rest of the cast is already in character, onstage or in the aisles of the audience. They encourage audience members to join their conga line dance to songs like LOVE ROLLERCOASTER by The Ohio Players. Once the conga line ends and the lights dim, all the inspectors stumble their way onstage and hold a contest singing OH, DANNY BOY. INSPECTOR MARY MELODY wins the contest. Applause.)

(Focus shifts to PATTY McKAY and MANNY MANDELBAUM. They sit at a table full of empty alcohol bottles, spilling over ashtrays and scrambled piles of playing cards, loose cash and drugs. The Locker Room is a surreal nightmare, not realistic. Bloody body parts spill out of lockers and dozens of clipboards holding accident reports litter the room. Both inspectors still wear dirty, bloody uniforms: white Lab Coats, Hardhats and Goggles. They acknowledge the audience as if fellow guests at their roast.)

INSPECTOR MANNY

Ladies and Gentlemen, Wise Guys and Wild Women: here's another Toast at the Roast for Mr. about to be fucking retired after sixty eight mother fucking years on the job...your partner in bribes and fines but never crimes...he's no longer our fucking bad ass of a boss as it's now fucking officially midnight...won't you join me in our 68th and fucking final hip hip hooray for Chief Inspector of Nothing Anymore: Mr. Patty McKay! Hip Hip Hooray! Patty McKay!

ALFIE BUNZ as Deputy Ride Inspector Manny Mandelbaum Saluting ZERO BOY as Chief Ride Inspector Patty McKay gives his last instructions upon retirement. Photo by Norman Blake.

INSPECTOR PATTY

(Head resting on table. He's wasted.)

Oh fucking forgetaboutit already you flattering assholes, I'm nodding out and I'm wasted... I'm hallucinating... I'm falling asleep...(hiccup) five more minutes maximum men or I'll be wobbling and weaving and sleepwalking home...

(Head hits table again.)

ALFIE BUNZ as Deputy Ride Inspector Manny Mandelbaum parties with Cocaine while ZERO BOY as retiring Chief Ride Inspector prefers getting drunk on Guinness, and NATI AMOS as another Ride Inspector lights a joint. Photo by Norman Blake.

INSPECTOR MANNY

What are you talking about this party's just needs refueling, Big Boss! *(he snorts a line of cocaine)* Oh how sweet it is Brooklyn! *(another line another nostril)* It's midnight we're bad ass Brooklyn ride inspectors let's tell fucked up true stories about tourists dying on fucked up amusement park rides! Horror stories Horror rides: Hip Hip Hooray! Hip Hip Hooray?

INSPECTOR PATTY

When Irish Eyes Are Blinking

And Sleep's A Yawn Away

Yours Truly Inspector Patty

Starts to Dream His Life

Away...women...whiskey...wages...

INSPECTOR MANNY

I swear to God these are true stories or my name isn't Deputy Chief Ride Inspector Manny Mendelbloom. A customer lost his head on the Jumbo Jet ride, another lost his hand on the Twister. Himalaya took a Life, Hell Hole cut off a leg. Bungie ride sliced a body in half. Giant Spider crushed a head.

INSPECTOR PATTY

I wrote the reports. No more reports.

INSPECTOR MANNY

One busy afternoon a car crashes into Nathan's some guy loses his arm while eating a hot-dog. I swear to God the severed arm still grasping the hot-dog flies through the air and lands on the grill.

INSPECTOR PATTY

I got no beef with Nathan's. No more reports...zzz...

INSPECTOR MANNY

A customer fell one hundred feet to his death off a Rainbow. A woman's hair was ripped out on the Go Kart track. One day the mechanical Fat Lady at the Magic Carpet Fun House rolled right out of her big window crashed right through the glass still laughing and cut up two people on line on the sidewalk below. Blood every fucking where!

INSPECTOR PATTY

zzz...I still lose sleep over those reports...Leering Lepricauns on Lucky Charms give me lesser nightmares No more reports... zzz...

INSPECTOR MANNY

A man gets dragged by a famous roller coaster that takes him around the first big turn and rips his arm off. The second turn takes his leg off and the third turn throws him out of his seat and fifty feet into the air... and this dude lives to tell about it! Big NY Post headline: Roller Coaster Amputee Roller Skates at Studio 54!

INSPECTOR PATTY

And that report Inspectors still touches me drunken old Irish heart so I'm retired and I'm out of here... I'm drunk... and falling asleep... Deputy Inspector Manny I leave you in charge and your final instructions are to pick me up, point me in the right direction... give me a swift kick in the ass out the door... and ask these kind people here to get up out of their seats and walk with me as we shut down this raunchy roast and find our wicked ways home...

SCENE TWO

(Ride Inspector Patty McKay sleepwalks, arms stretched out... There is a sound loop recording playing over and over of a manual typewriter. Smoke and Fire Effects. Panic. Screams. PATTY bumbles with a large file folder.)

PATTY TALKS AS HE HAND WRITES

Accident Report. By Rookie Ride Inspector Patrick McKay. Location: Luna Park Surf Avenue, West 12th to West 8th Street. Ride: Every damn one. Category: Total Death and Destruction. Accident Details: My first fucking day on the job and forty fucked rides burn up in fire. I've never seen dead bodies before no less smelled burnt ones...I pissed in my pants then I puked what do you guys expect from a 17 year old rookie? You guys laughed at me and said "Patty, if you wanna get along just start drinking and swearing on the job like everyone else-

(The other INSPECTORS echo and taunt him with those very same words.)

So here goes guys: WHAT THE FUCK! But it's all Blarney Bullshit to me!

(The Additional RIDE INSPECTORS whisper to the audience about horrific and traumatic accidents they have witnessed.)

SCENE THREE

(The set fills with an army of blood soaked dolls as if a mass murderer had just happened within It's A Small World After All. We hear a broadcast of TV Breaking News.)

PATTY RECORDS ON A DICTAPHONE

Accident Report. Location: New York World's Fair. Flushing Queens. Pepsi-Cola Pavilion. Ride: Boat ride by Disney. It's A Small World After All. Category: Top Secret. Handle with care. Special Attention for your eyes only Commissioner Robert Moses. Accident Details: Accident? What accident? Remarks: Dear Moses, thank you for reading me your personal ten commandments of loyalty and enlightening me on my path to promotion. Please thank Walt and tell him that the wife and kid are excited about next week's vacation in California.

SCENE FOUR

(Ride Inspector PATTY MCKAY sleepwalks, arms stretched out... he leads the audience to a flooded vision of Astroland. The extra RIDE INSPECTORS have water pistols to use on audience.)

PATTY RECORDS ON HIS SMART PHONE

Accident Report Location: The ENTIRE Fucking Island. Ride...no, rides...no, Every fucking one's in danger. Category: Hurricane Gloria on the horizon People say Gentrification is Coming but forget about it as the flood's coming first! Water parks are the more likely future...Potential Accident Details: Evacuation Orders should be issued ASAP before she submerges ...north shore and south shore...water to the left of me water to the right of me Mermaid to Neptune I'm ordering a total evacuation except for Astroland's Diving Bell and Waterflume...at least Astroland's waterproof... fireproof...Astroland will never go under..lglub-blub...never go under...Abandon Ship... MayDay... SOS... we're about to go under...

SCENE FIVE

(Ride Inspector PATTY MCKAY sleepwalks, arms stretched out to a roller coaster accident. The extra RIDE INSPECTORS bark like homeless dogs)

PATTY SHOOTS A VIDEO REPORT

Accident Report Location: Maybe it's Surf and West 15th and maybe it's Bowery and West 16th - Giuliani doesn't give a fuck. Ride: Thunderbolt. Category: Inactive Roller Coaster closed for 20 years. Accident Details: Could not gain access due to locked perimeter fence, guard dogs and Bensonhurst born caretaker. First impression: No accident. No change in condition. Ride remains closed and some distance from property line fence with no structural danger to public. Remarks: City Hall wants to beautiful the neighborhood so here's my second opinion from a block away with toy binoculars I bought at a souvenir stand (receipt attached for reimbursement). On second thought this ride represents the #1 danger to the public good in Brooklyn. I hereby recommend an Emergency Demolition Order - Arrest the caretaker, shoot the guard dogs and bulldoze the roller coaster tomorrow morning 6 AM and if the owner finds out and sends a lawyer with a cease and desist, put a fucking bullet in his back and bury him under the mother fucking Boardwalk.

(The audience encounters ZOMBIE RIDE INSPECTORS...who gather them together facing a chicken wire cage with an accident survivor played by STICKY FINGERS who wears an Arm Brace. She has a can and begs money...sometimes in and sometimes out of her cage. Meanwhile the other ZOMBIE RIDE INSPECTORS have sex and screw each other admidst ruins and weeds.)

STICKY FINGERS

I'm just a girl who needs money you should give me some cash...I'm a coaster crash survivor give me some money and I'll sing you a song... find some loose change in your pocket and buy a ride ticket from me I don't care if the coaster is broken. I don't care if you already paid in full for this horror show as I haven't gotten my cut yet. I always get my cut and that gave me my name: I'M SUZY STICKY FINGERS Thank you, sir and thank you mam. Step right up and buy a ticket and see for yourself... nothing's wrong with this ride... nothing's wrong with this ride... no reason to kill it...

(STICKY FINGERS herds INSPECTOR PATTY inside her GoGo Cage as well. She sings and dances.)

You saved my life... I'm Your Groupie... You're my Hero Ride Inspector in a Bloody White uniform...You saved a few of my fingers...You want a really cool hand job Inspector? ...ha-haha...

SCENE SIX

(Audience suddenly in complete darkness.)

RECORDING (SIRI Voice)

Accident Report Location: Brighton Beach. Oceanview Avenue. Ride: No ride. My bungalow, my house. Category: My family. The wife and the kid. Accident Details: My bad habits... my selfish lifestyle... but that's all gonna change now... gonna change now because today I'm retired. Remarks: Maybe I should buy her flowers... maybe roses and champagne and chocolates... maybe I'm gonna get some from the wife... just get back and make it all up to the Mary McKay and the kid...

(The Door suddenly opens and reveals a room full of power saws and dismembered limbs. His wife is crying and rocking a dead baby back and forth in her arms.)

WIFE/MARY MELODY

Your own son is dead on that dark ride you signed off on this morning so don't think you're gonna get some as I'm no longer your redheaded Mary McKay you murdering motherfucker I'm PROUD MARY the Tina Turner Acid Queen Black Irish version of your wife and I'm about to kick your ass for killing my baby! Like you stuck a knife in my heart. . .as if you tied up your own son Isaac and lifted his body onto a table saw and sliced my heart up like this!

(She sings as she saws.)

Hush, little baby, don't say a word,

Mama's going to buy you a mockingbird.

If that mockingbird won't sing...

(sob)... I... I...

Mama's going to buy you a private eye.

If that private eye don't work,

Mama's going to buy you a state supreme court clerk.

If that clerk can't deliver the judge,

Mama's going to buy you some guys with a grudge.

If those goons can't get revenge,

Mama's going to squeal to the press instead.

If mommy stumbles and falls to the ground,

You'll still be the sweetest little boy in town.

So hush little baby, don't you cry,

Daddy loves you and so do I.

After the cops drove me home from the morgue they handed me a sealed envelope a really thick sealed unmarked envelope and they said it was for you . . . Patty McKay you know we were both hoping for a fat bundle of cash the day you retired. . . so I opened it. . .you were served with a subpoena . . . the cops have been waiting outside and they need to take you to court...

(Lots of loud police whistles AND FLASHING LIGHTS.)

PRINCESS PAT as Mary McKay, wife of the Inspector. She mourns their Dead Baby. Photo by Norman Blake.

SCENE SEVEN

(Ride Inspector PATTY MCKAY sleepwalks, arms stretched out...is led to a courtroom The audience is seated on benches.)

DEAD BODY INSPECTOR/THE JUDGE

Hear ye, Hear ye, the court's in session. I am the judge. And you are the jury. My jury my court room my rules. Please rise and raise your right hand... (not YOU Inspector)... jurors, repeat after m e:

I pledge allegiance to the creeps

That hold court in Kings County

And to the things of which dreams are made of

One Nightmare Under Indigestion

With snorers in horror for all!

Thank you, be seated... not you Inspector you are now going to face judgment on a ride I call The Guillotine.. Verdict first, trial later. Juror One, please stand. The defendant has been charged with multiple counts of DWI: DREAMING WHILE INTOXICATED! Dreaming...while intoxicate d...hiccup... intoxicated...snoring? Innocent or Guilty? Be seated. Juror Two, Innocent or Guilty? Say what, I guess Juror Two doesn't speak English and is dismissed. Guilty! Be seated. Juror Three, Guilty or Guilty? Be seated. Juror Four, have you ever had a nightmare? Dismissed, guilty!... (etc.)

Ladies and Gentlemen, you have found the Defendant GUILTY and I hereby sentence Chief Ride Inspector Patty McKay to death by taking a ride on the Guillotine. Inspector, do you have any last words?

ZERO BOY as Ride Inspector Patty McKay put on trial by PATRICK SALAZAR as the Angel of Death. Photo by Norman Blake.

INSPECTOR

Pint a Guinness might be nice...

(THE JUDGE throws the switch and the blade falls however Inspector's head is still attached.)

What the fuck! Something's wrong...

(JUDGE pokes INSPECTOR who awakes and jumps out of the device.)

PATRICK SALAZAR as the Angel of Death judges the life of Chief Ride Inspector, Patty McKay played by ZERO BOY. Photo by Norman Blake.

INSPECTOR PATTY

What the fuck! Judge, you need an emergency inspection from the Death Sentence Division... besides, EVERYONE knows you can't die in your own dream... Ladies and Gentlemen, the rides in Coney Island are safe... nobody dies in the end... except for an occasional audience member at this Creepshow...

(Coming at audience.)

hahaha... have fun... hahaha...on the safe rides...

THE END

PATRICK SALAZAR as Angel of Death puts ZERO BOY's head.into the Guillotine playing Ride Inspector Patty McKay. Photo by Norman Blake

About the author

In 1979 DICK D. ZIGUN proclaimed himself the Permanently UnElected Mayor of Coney Island. He created the MERMAID PARADE, founded a landmark arts center, started a museum, revived circus sideshows and ran a theater company where he developed two dozen Weird American Plays. Outside of Brooklyn, his scripts have been produced by the Mark Taper Forum, Repertory Theater of St. Louis, People's Light and Theatre Company, Eureka Theatre, Bridge Street Theatre, LaMaMa, Theater for The New City, West Bank Café, Webster Hall, Franklin Furnace and The Clemente. He is an Alumni of Yale School of Drama, New Dramatists and Bennington College. He is a member of the Burlesque Hall of Fame and the People's Hall of Fame and received a NYC Acker Award for avant-garde excellence. Zigun has also received a NYSCA Playwriting Grant and 2 NYFA Playwriting Fellowships.

DICK D. ZIGUN in performance. Photo by Norman Blake.

Please watch for his next book, coming soon: *Impossible to Produce Plays: 7 Banned or Bizarre Dramas.*

About the Photographers

Norman Blake

Pages: 15, 16, 23, 32, 46, 47, 51, 52, 79, 81, 113, 114, 120, 125, 149, 150, 156, 158, 159, and 161.

A Brooklyn-based photographer, Norman Blake began his career immediately after high school in 1973 and later graduated from the Germain School of Photography. His early work focused on automotive drag racing, contributing to national magazines like *Super Stock & Drag* Illustrated and *Drag Racing USA*. Blake's diverse portfolio includes concert and street photography, as well as commissioned projects. Currently, he serves as the house photographer for Coney Island USA, a nonprofit arts organization, capturing events such as the Mermaid Parade, CI film festival, Burlesque at the Beach, and Sideshow performances, alongside documenting the vibrant happenings of Coney Island with his trusty Nikon camera.

OTHER PHOTO CREDITS FROM THE COLLECTION OF THE CONEY ISLAND MUSEUM

Costa Mantis

Pages: 130 and 131.

Cynthia Freedman

Pages: 139, 142, and 143.

Evelyn Zigun

Pages: 136 and 145.

READ MORE!

http://outsidetalkerpress.com

www.ingramcontent.com/pod-product-compliance
Ingram Content Group UK Ltd.
Pitfield, Milton Keynes, MK11 3LW, UK
UKHW061134310726
14090UKWH00038B/1464